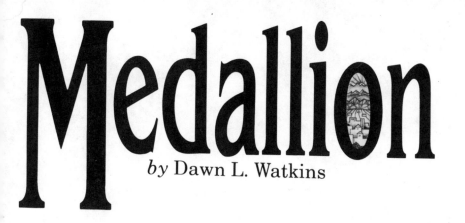

Medallion

by Dawn L. Watkins

A fantasy for young readers

for grade four

Designed for use with *READING for Christian Schools® 4* and
for the reading enjoyment of children of comparable ages

Bob Jones University Press, Greenville, South Carolina 29614

Medallion

Edited by E. Anne Smith
Illustrated by Dana Thompson
Cover illustration by Del Thompson

©1985 by Bob Jones University Press
Greenville, South Carolina 29614

ISBN 0-89084-282-5
Printed in the United States of America

20   19   18   17

Contents

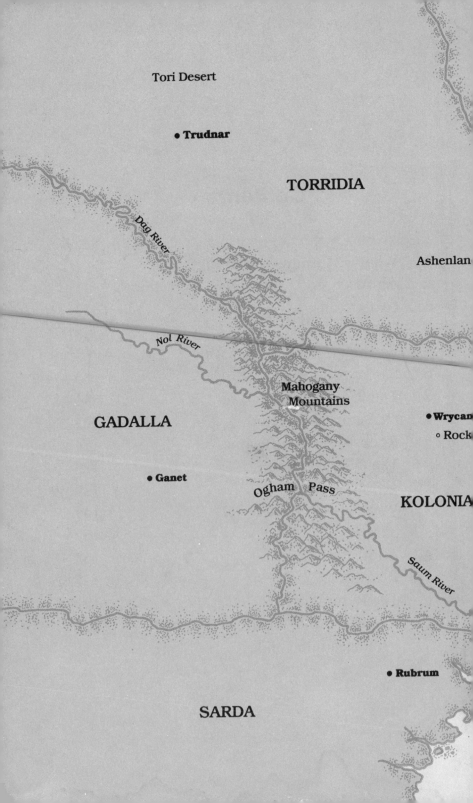

Clar Plains

KAPNOS

Regner River

DIDER

Cordus

Valor River

Lapis •

Brass
Mountains

Plains of Fidere

Torus
Point

Rudus Desert

Blee Bog

Saz River

Skreel Forest

LITORIS

• Brankus

Malus Sea

KAPNOS and the UNDER COUNTRIES

CHAPTER 1

What A Morning May Bring Forth

"Umbo! Return!"

The great white owl made a sweeping arc high in the air and came round toward his master.

Trave stood squinting in the morning sun, his right arm straight out from his shoulder and his feet spread solidly beneath him. The boy followed the bird's sweep with pleasure, a pleasure that put color in his handsome face. Trave had the fine, straight nose and the high, ruddy cheeks of the Gadallans. He might have been any common boy training his pet on a windy hill. But his rings, wide bands of gold set with gems, showed that he was not.

"Return," Trave called again, and he slapped the thick leather cuff strapped to his arm.

The owl slowed his glide with two lazy flaps of his wings. Then the bird put out his talons as if he would catch a mouse or a rabbit, flung his wings up, and dropped toward the boy's arm.

Umbo landed gracefully, barely clutching the leather cuff, but his weight made Trave stagger back and crook his arm in. Umbo fluttered briefly, gaining his hold.

"Well done, Umbo." The boy stroked the rich feathers, smiling. Reaching into the pouch slung over his neck, Trave tore a piece of meat off for the owl. "Good boy."

A steady wind buffeted the hill and passed on into the valley, down to the capital city of Ganet. The gold dome of the palace gleamed among the white marble buildings like a small sun.

Trave let Umbo fly to his perch, and then he gazed down into the valley.

"This is my kingdom, Umbo. Ganet is my city." He swung back toward the bird. "And I will be king here!"

His voice carried loudly across the wind and echoed *here, here* in the woods behind. Umbo gazed at his master, blinked once, slowly, and pecked at a wing feather.

"I will," said the boy, unbuckling his cuff.

In a while Trave started down the hill, his gear neatly hung about him. His well-woven gloves with smooth leather cuffs hung over his belt. In one hand he carried a loosely braided thong. He glanced casually back to see if Umbo followed.

As he did, the owl raised his wide wings and lifted soundlessly off the perch, catching a current and rising into the morning.

Trave walked on, flicking the thong into his other palm. The wild flowers of the kingdom of Gadalla nodded their heavy heads in the wind. Trave nodded back, as a king would when he passed among his subjects. A sweet scent rose from the purple, red, and yellow flowers and carried on the air.

All at once the boy threw out the thong, high and away.

"Attack!" he called.

Umbo surged upward for two mighty strokes of his wings. Then he folded his wings close and soared downward, a shrill screech vibrating the air.

Like a white-hot arrow he came down, beautiful against the blue sky and the green Gadallan hills. He caught up the braid from the tall grass without brushing the ground and rose skyward with it in his talon.

"Splendid!" said Trave. "Bring it to me."

Umbo flew back toward the forest.

"Here!" said Trave. "Come here!"

The owl wheeled about, screeching.

"Come here!" The boy's face got red. "Here, I say!"

Dangling the thong, Umbo dipped and charged about on the wind. Then he passed directly over Trave and dropped the leather.

The boy snatched it up and walked on.

"No meat for disobedient birds."

Umbo swooped low, making a little clicking sound. He flew close to Trave a few seconds and then made a circle.

"It's no good, Umbo."

The bird came back, casting a shadow ahead of Trave, but the boy did not look up. Finally Umbo landed beside his master and hopped awkwardly along.

"Oh, very well," said the boy, stopping and putting his fists on his hips. "I forgive you."

Umbo took a little run and climbed the air again.

"But no meat," Trave called after him.

It was nearly noon when Trave entered the gates of Ganet.

"Good day, Prince Trave," said the gatekeeper.

"Good day." Trave's copper hair shone in the sun.

"Would Your Highness prefer a carriage? It is a long walk to the palace."

"No, thank you," said the prince. "I would prefer a horse."

"It is forbidden, Your Highness. King Panii said—"

"I quite remember what Panii said: 'No horses for the prince.' He fears me, that is it!" Trave wanted the gatekeeper to agree, but the man offered his suggestion again.

"But a carriage is—"

"I'll walk," said Trave.

The gatekeeper bowed. "I understand your grace's desire for a horse. I was once a horseman myself."

Trave stood silent a moment. "It is Panii's rules—not you—making me angry. When I am king, I will have many horses—and you shall be the groom of my horse, the king's horse."

The gatekeeper looked up briefly with a hopeful smile but quickly dropped his gaze.

Trave went on, thoughtfully, tying Umbo's practice thong around his wrist.

Carts and wagons jostled along in the streets. Dogs and little children raced among the market stands and up the steps of the stone buildings. Women called to each other over piles of tapestries and silks. Older children played a game with bright, clear red stones that in less wealthy countries might have been used as money.

The day was hot now, and Trave stopped under a stone arch to watch a man make a wheel. The man lifted something that looked like a small barrel, drilled with holes around the middle. Into one of the holes he fitted a tapered spoke and pounded it snug with a heavy hammer.

The man, young and tanned, pounded another spoke into the thick hub and then looked up.

"Hello, boy," he said.

Trave pushed away from the arch wall and straightened his shoulders. His mouth was set in a fine line.

"I am Trave, Prince of Gadalla."

"Excuse me, Prince," said the wheelwright, picking up another spoke. "I did not know you—but I have heard of you."

"Oh?"

"Indeed. I am from Kolonia. All outsiders who trade in Gadalla must sign a border pass. Your name is on the passes—under King Panii's."

"Only that," said Trave. "Only border passes."

The man studied the end of the spoke and fitted it into a hole in the wheel's center.

"What is the Prince of Gadalla doing out in the streets?" he asked.

"I go where I choose," said Trave.

"A prince's privilege, certainly."

"Why are you out of Kolonia?"

"Gadalla needs wheels. Kolonia does not need any more wheelwrights. So I come here."

He tapped the spoke to straighten it slightly.

"A wheelwright's privilege, certainly," said Trave.

The man laughed heartily. "How old are you, Prince of Gadalla, that you fence so well with words?"

"Old enough to be king."

The man stopped his work, looking directly at Trave. Trave looked directly back.

"Panii is king," said the craftsman at last.

"Until I am." Trave's eyes did not leave the Kolonian.

"As you say, Prince. I am only a stranger here. Your ways are unknown to me."

Trave looked away and watched the carts in the street. Then he turned back to the wheelwright.

"Tell me of your Kolonia. Does it look like Gadalla?"

"Kolonia is a land of skillful craftsmen. And music and stories." The man put down his hammer and spoke eagerly. "When you cross the Mahogany Mountains or go through the pass, you come to the beautiful plains—you should see." He turned, smiling, to the prince.

"What kind of music?" asked Trave.

"Ah. Songs and old tunes played on instruments made hundreds of years ago."

Trave listened, interested.

"What is the strangest thing in Kolonia?"

The man cocked his head a little and thought. "Well," he said at last, "that would be Nog."

"Nog?"

"An outlander who lives under a bog."

"Why does he live in a bog?" Trave asked.

"Not *in—under*," said the man. "I don't know, for sure. No one my age has seen him. He went under a long time ago. But stories say he hates the greed and war he found above the bog."

"Hmmm," said Trave. "What else do you know?"

But the man only laughed and shook his head, "Not much."

Trave smiled a little and stayed a minute more. "Good day, wheelwright. You are welcome in Gadalla," he said finally.

"Good day, Prince Trave," answered the young man. "Live long and well."

Trave walked again amid the crowds. The man bent to his wheel.

"That is the prince?" said a voice from the other side of the arch.

"So he said," the wheelwright answered, studying the speaker.

The voice belonged to a tall, handsome soldier who wore thick leather leggings and iron-soled boots. He drummed his gloved fingers on the hilt of his sword and watched Trave weave through the market.

Then he turned back to the wheelwright.

"You are his friend?"

The craftsman's eyes narrowed. "You are a Sardan."

The soldier chortled in his throat. "An intelligent Kolonian. What a wonder."

"You are a Sardan who yet lives in my presence— a greater wonder!"

"Bold for a Kolonian," said the other.

"Remember what you learned from Kolonia in the Gadallan Wars!" said the wheelwright, standing and picking up his hammer.

"Aha, ha, ha," laughed the Sardan, going back the way he had come.

Along the street and down side avenues, Gadallan merchants called to passersby. "Imported," they cried, holding up silver goblets and handsomely carved trays.

———

Trave scanned the sky for Umbo. He caught sight of the bird far to the east. He'll come when he's hungry, thought Trave.

The prince stepped into the palace stables. It was cool and dim there and usually quiet, except for the pawing and snorting of the horses.

He hung up his pouch, his cuff, his gloves, and the thong. He threw what little meat was left in the pouch to the stable dog and then stood in the doorway, not wanting to go into the palace.

Toward the stable from the palace came the stable master, leading a great gray horse, perfectly brushed and trimmed and harnessed in a way Trave had never seen before. Three shiny leather straps were laid across the horse's rump, held to a high-seated saddle with two narrow straps running forward to the chest plate.

Trave hurried out to stop the stable master.

"Whose animal is this?" His eyes were full of admiration and his voice full of curiosity.

"A visiting king's, Your Highness."

"Who?"

"Gris, King of Kapnos and the North."

"Why has he come?"

"I do not know, Prince Trave. I have charge only of the stables."

"What a splendid horse," said the boy, running his hand down the broad neck and one heavily muscled shoulder. The animal's thick mane was cut evenly and braided partway down the neck.

"I've never seen one finer," said the stable master.

Despite the heat and the large saddle and the weighty flank shields, the horse stood calmly, neither pawing nor tossing.

"What is he called?" asked Trave.

"Cene, Your Highness. The King of Kapnos says the word means *brave* in his tongue."

"He looks like a brave horse," said the Prince.

The stable master led the horse on, and Trave watched. The polished leather shone like metal; the horse's gait was true and flawless, the back hooves landing squarely in the prints of the front hooves.

Then Trave was off to the palace to see the owner of such a beast.

The reception room was hung with purple tapestries and mirrors. Every window and door was swung open, letting sunlight into the farthest corners. Trave was amazed at the beauty of the room now. Panii rarely allowed it open or even had the draperies pulled back. The sun slanted in on white marble floors and glowed on the brass handles of the doors and the fittings of the windows. Cedar beams across the vaulted ceiling were set with bright gems the size of walnuts.

Panii sat as if he had been plopped into his gold chair by some giant child, who had used him as a doll and had tired of him. Many red and purple cushions surrounded him, and two ladies stood by to fan him with huge balla leaves. Trave flushed with anger to see his uncle's fat ankles propped on a stool that had belonged to Trave's mother.

And then he saw Gris. Surely it was Gris, for the man stood in the vast hall with all the presence and dignity of a king.

He was tall, much taller than Panii or any of his guards, and was clad in fine-mesh mail. He wore black leather boots that rose just past the knee, charcoal leggings that had no seams, and a smooth silver belt that buckled on the side. From a leather belt that hung below the silver one slanted a scabbard of black onyx with silver tip and trim. His shirt had full white sleeves and a high collar, which stood up from the mail vest. He carried a silver and onyx helmet under his left arm and a pair of mesh and leather gloves in his right hand. A gray cloak hung down from his left shoulder to the top of his boot.

"Excuse the heat," Panii was saying. "There is little we can do about it." He laughed at his little joke. "Are you thirsty?"

Before the guest could answer, Panii motioned his servant away. "Go on—get some refreshment for our visiting king."

Trave stood beside a column near the back of the hall, unnoticed and unsummoned. He wanted to see Gris's face, but he dared not stir.

"Well, how may Gadalla serve you?" said Panii. He waved his hands around as he spoke, supposing it gave his words power.

"I have come to warn you of the Dark Alliance," said the foreign ruler. His voice, calm and clear, filled the hall and rang out in the colonnade even though the doors were open to the outside.

"Oh, bah," said Panii. "Gadalla is for Gadalla. Warn us of what?"

Panii's thready voice died out. Everyone in the great hall listened to hear Gris's next words.

"You cannot be neutral forever," the voice came forth. "Sarda will force you to choose."

"Sarda cannot force me to do anything. Neither can you." Panii turned his face away from Gris and gazed out a window.

Gris spoke again. "In these five years since the Gadallan Wars, the Sardans have built up their army again. They eye your wealthy kingdom. They study your strengths—and your weaknesses."

Panii continued to stare out the window. Trave saw two guards on either side of Panii glance at each other as if they knew these words to be true.

"Sarda is allied with Torridia and Litoris. Can you fight this Dark Alliance alone?" The King of Kapnos waited for an answer, but Panii only waggled his foot impatiently.

"Kapnos, Kolonia, and Dider would like to avoid another war, Panii," said Gris. "There will be a council at Wrycan of Kolonia."

At last Panii brought his fat face around to the visiting king. "You talk of things that are not nor cannot be. Gadalla is neutral." He smoothed the sleeve of his silk robe.

"In such a pass as this," said Gris, "to be neutral is to side with Sarda."

"Gadalla is for Gadalla, I tell you!" Panii yelled. "You want our gems and gold as much as you say your enemies do. You've wasted your breath and your time. I'll not be tricked."

Gris neither moved nor spoke.

Trave realized for the first time that the King of Kapnos had pure white hair.

"Well," said Panii, glancing back at Gris, "what keeps you? We are finished."

"You are finished," said Gris.

"And what is that?" said Panii, leaping up from his pillowed seat. "A threat?"

"A conclusion," said the other king.

"Get out! Guards!"

Panii's guards unsheathed their swords but did not come forward.

"Guards!" bawled Panii.

Gris held the guards back with a look. "Beware of Sarda. That is my only word. Remember their savage ways, Panii. They will take all Gadalla while you sit at your supper." Panii looked as if he might burst apart with rage.

"Seize him!" said Panii.

But the soldiers stood by as Gris turned to leave the hall.

As the old king turned, he saw Trave. He looked at the boy as if he knew him. He passed by the prince without a word, without changing his stride, but Trave felt as though Gris knew all about him.

Panii ranted at his guards who still held their swords. He threw down the drinks that the servant had brought.

Trave melted unobserved out of the hall. He could remember only the blue eyes that had looked keenly into his. And he knew that he had to talk to this king.

———

CHAPTER 2

An Afternoon Can Change Everything

Gris did not ask for his horse to be brought to him but went to the stables himself. Trave followed, a short way back.

A stable man was just beginning to remove the saddle when the king arrived.

"Thank you, young man," said Gris from the doorway. "But I will do that."

"Sir," said the groom, bowing. "I am sorry. What have I done wrong?"

"Why, not a thing," said the big man. "I simply did not want to add to your work."

"It is a pleasure to attend this horse, your lordship." The groom stroked the thick mane admiringly.

"If it is a pleasure to you, then," said Gris, stepping in to lift the saddle down for the groom. "Rather heavy, son. I'll get it."

The old man swung the saddle down to the tack rail as though it were a blanket. He shook it once and all the trim fell evenly into place along the rail.

"There," he said. "Give him a good brushing."

Trave stood outside, trying to decide what he would say.

The King of Kapnos turned toward the door.

"Trave, is it?"

The prince felt his heart jump, but he made no outward sign.

"I am Trave, Prince of Gadalla."

The old man nodded and smiled.

"You may rest your horse as long as you like," Trave said, not coming in.

"Thank you, Prince Trave. There is much hospitality for horses in Gadalla, I see."

"You are welcome, too, King of Kapnos."

The foreigner walked out into the bright day. Light shone out from the silver on his clothes. He put out his hand to Trave.

Trave took it and shook it once, manfully.

"How do you know me?" the boy asked.

"I knew your father."

Trave felt as though he had suddenly fallen into a hot spring during a cold rain.

"My father?"

"Dokos, the greatest of all Gadallan kings. He was my friend."

Trave could barely keep from running about the stable yard, yelling for joy. But he remembered that he was a prince, and thus he only reached forward to grasp the old king's arm.

"Tell me!"

Panii had refused to let Dokos's name be spoken since he had become ruler. Trave remembered little about his father, and he had been forbidden to ask about him.

"Come," said the boy. "Come to the west meadow where we may speak."

Walking calmly and evenly as men who have learned much of the world do, the king followed the boy to the meadow. They came to a clearing circled by bluegreen wincha trees.

"Now," said Trave. "Tell me of my father!"

"What would you know?" asked Gris.

"How long was he king?"

"Seventeen years."

"Did he tell you about me?"

Gris smiled kindly. "I heard about Trave many times."

The boy felt a warmth spread over him as though the sun had moved out from behind a cloud.

Trave asked, "How did you know him?"

"Your father came to Kapnos when he was a young man, not much older than you. He asked Kapnos to join with him against Sarda. We were allies and friends from then on. Your father and I fought together in the Great Gadallan wars. He led a mighty army into the last battle—and he won."

"But he died there too," said Trave.

"Yes. He died," said Gris. He said the words so gently that Trave felt as if the king had put his hand on his shoulder. But Gris had not moved.

"Do I look like him?" the boy asked.

"You do."

Again, Trave was quiet. He looked at the leather cuffs of his breeches that were just above his boots.

"Was he a good king?" he asked presently.

"He was good," said Gris, "and therefore he was great."

They had sat down under thick wincha trees where the air was cooler and sweet.

"What did he do that was great?" Trave's head held more questions than could be asked in three afternoons.

"He was true to his word; he was careful of his people; he made everyone in Gadalla learn to read."

Trave was a little disappointed with the last statement.

"Was he a great warrior?" he asked before Gris could go on.

"When he had to be. He was brave in peace as well as in war."

"Kings should be warriors," said the prince.

"Kings must be many things," said Gris.

"I will be king of Gadalla. I will be a king like my father."

Gris watched the boy but made no comment.

"My uncle is not a king. He is a cheat, a fake. I am the king! And he treats me worse than a servant! I am not permitted to sit on a horse, eat at the king's table, or even speak my father's name!"

Trave jumped up and paced away as he spoke. "You are a ruler—tell me, who is more fit to reign— Panii or me?"

Gris looked steadily at Trave. "What makes a ruler fit to rule?"

"Courage," said Trave. "And strength."

"Then many captains might be kings."

"True kings are born to rule. They own the right."

The old king looked away into the woods across the field. A light wind came up. He sat with his elbows on his knees, hands clasped before him.

"Will you help me get my throne?" Trave said at last.

"I may be able to help you," said the man in gray, turning his keen gaze back to the prince.

"Good." There was a pause, a bit too long. "I am grateful."

The king stood up, his mail chinking almost inaudibly and falling in fine creases from his shoulders. "But answer me this—"

Trave waited.

"What is a king's first duty?"

From far away and long ago, Trave could remember his father's voice, always a quiet voice, telling him of a king's duties.

"To learn what is true," said the prince.

"Ah." Gris smiled. "You are your father's son. Come, I have much to tell you."

Trave followed the old king.

"Your father," said the king, "led a mighty army of many faithful men into the last battle. When he saw that he would die of his wounds, he called his best captains to him and told them that he had given his royal medallion to one of the men who had fought beside him."

Trave's gaze never left the face of the king.

"He made them promise," said Gris, "made them give their word as Gadallan soldiers, to follow the man who would wear the medallion into the Great Hall of Gadalla. There are many brave Gadallans who yet wait for such a man."

The prince's eyes grew large and bright. "Who has my father's medallion?"

Gris went on. "Whoever has the medallion will control the armies and the court."

"Do you know where it is?" Trave's muscles were tight with excitement.

"Yes."

"Can you get it for me?"

Gris shook his head. "Your father's last words were these: 'The man worthy to be king will have to come by it nobly.' It is not a thing to be gotten lightly."

"I will get it," said the prince. "Where do I begin?"

Gris had stopped walking, and the two stood in the middle of the meadow.

"I will lead you. But you must be willing to follow. It will be no easy journey—it will be dangerous and wild, going through such places as are not dreamed of in Gadalla."

"I care not."

"You may get hurt. I cannot say."

Trave did not slack. "I will go."

"Good," said Gris, with a tone that seemed to say some great matter had been decided.

They started back the way they had come.

"Did you know my mother too?" Trave could remember nothing about her.

"Yes. She was a beautiful, gracious lady, Trave. Always laughing, always sending her servants out so she could cook for your father herself."

Trave trotted to keep up. "Was she a good cook?"

"That she was," said Gris.

Trave realized suddenly that he was hungry. "I will order food brought to us at the palace."

"There is time to eat later. Do you want to be king or not?"

Trave made no answer, but he wondered to himself whether all kings went without lunch.

Gris strode on, with the prince managing to keep abreast.

They came again to the stables.

"We leave now," said the king.

"Now? I'm not ready."

"Make ready."

Trave hesitated. "I have a bird. Umbo."

"Is he trained?"

"Well, mostly."

"Let's see him, then."

Trave climbed a rail and gave a long, lilting whistle. He waited, and whistled again.

The old man and the boy scanned the heavens. Trave feared that Umbo would be in one of his independent moods and fail to come.

But presently the owl came soaring down from the west hills, smoothly and silently.

"An owl," said Gris, a trace of wonder in his strong voice.

"My uncle forbids anyone but himself to have falcons and eagles. They are king's birds, he says."

"Have you trained him to hunt by day?" asked the king.

"I had to," said Trave. "I am kept under guard at night."

"Umbo is a fine fellow. Bring him along."

Trave was pleased. Umbo flew overhead, casting his wide shadow over Trave.

"Watch," said the boy. He pulled a strap from his boot and threw it in an *S* on the ground. "Attack!"

Umbo flew up and dived downward like a stream of light, pouncing on the strap and lifting off again in one clean sweep.

"I'm teaching him to go only for snakes."

Gris regarded the boy as if he had said a remarkable thing, but answered nothing.

Umbo dropped the strap at Trave's feet and then settled onto a fence rail.

"Good boy," said Trave. "Lots of food for you tonight." He smoothed the delicate feathers under the owl's neck.

"Do you have a horse?" asked Gris.

Trave answered wearily, "No."

"Do you know anything of riding?"

Trave could not answer. He had sometimes sat upon the horses when no one was in the stables. He had watched the stable masters exercise Panii's horses. But he could not bring himself to say he had never ridden.

"You may choose a horse at my camp," said Gris. "I will see that you learn to ride."

The boy could not be sure whether he felt more gratitude or humiliation.

"It is no shame to be untaught," said Gris. "Just to be unlearned. Now, get a cloak and tell your uncle you go with me."

"No!"

Gris raised his eyebrows, but his kindly expression did not change.

"I mean," said Trave, "he will forbid me."

"Tell him," said Gris. "But give no reason."

To Trave's surprise, Panii did not forbid him to leave. Rather, he seemed happy.

"Yes, boy. Go. Go seek your fortune in the vast world. A prince should travel around, get an education. Yes, go on."

Then he turned back to the laden table and took another slab of meat.

Trave told Gris how Panii had spoken.

"He thinks you will not return," said the king, buckling the big saddle on Cene. "I expect he does not know about the medallion. Your father's soldiers would not speak of it, except among themselves."

For the first time, Trave felt a pang of fear. He wavered an instant in his resolution.

"You will ride behind me on Cene for now," Gris was saying. "Do you have fowling gear to take?"

Trave shook out of his daze. "Just these." He took down his gloves, his cuff, his pouch, and the thong and hung them neatly around himself. He threw the cloak over his arm.

"Wait!" he said. "I need meat for Umbo."

He returned shortly to find Gris and Cene waiting.

"The day closes," said the king. "Let us move."

He hoisted Trave onto the flank guards behind the saddle, and before Trave could say he was ready, the long journey had begun.

They passed through Ganet toward the gates. Cene's gait was steady and smooth.

"See how I sit in the saddle? See how the heels are carried low in the rings? Watch and learn," Gris said over his shoulder.

Trave studied every move the old horseman made. He wanted to learn to ride well as quickly as he could.

The markets had cleared out a little. Children still ran among the wagons and down the alleys, but in fewer numbers. The dogs dozed in patches of sun. There was little chatter now.

The little company passed under the arch where the Kolonian had been forming a wheel. He was gone and so were his tools. Trave looked back for him and caught sight of a soldier in heavy boots looking at

Gris from the shadows. He wore a massive helmet with an iron snake head on it. The man disappeared like a mist.

"Sir," said Trave. "There was a man in the archway. Hiding, I think."

"Probably," said Gris.

"Shouldn't we see?"

"No need to look for trouble. If it is ours, it will find us."

Trave considered the words in silence. They passed through the last of the market.

"The forge used to be over there," said Gris, nodding toward an old stone building.

"There was a forge? We have no forge now. We buy what we need from the traders."

"Yes," was all the king said.

Two girls were playing on the steps of an inn. The bigger one had long, thick braids that whipped out behind her when she jumped down the stairs. She stopped, laughing, and leaned against the slanting stair wall.

A sudden shadow passed over the girls, and Trave recognized it too late.

"No," he shouted. "No—Umbo, go back!" But Umbo made a dive for one of the golden braids.

The girls screamed and ran up the stairs. Umbo missed his target and seemed puzzled. He banked in the air for another pass.

By now Trave had jumped down into the street. "No! Umbo, no!"

The owl hovered briefly and then flapped far up above the building.

"I'm sorry," Trave said to the girl with braids. "It was a mistake."

She looked as if she couldn't decide whether to cry or to scold. She stayed tight against the wall.

"He'll never do it again." Trave wanted her to say something. "He's not a bad owl."

She only looked at him with wide eyes and nodded slowly.

"We'll take him away with us," said Gris. "And teach him better manners."

The girl lifted her gaze to Gris and smiled faintly. Gris gave her a rich smile.

"That's a girl," said the king. "Come on, Trave. You've work to do."

The prince climbed back up behind Gris, and Cene walked on.

The blond-haired girl with long braids lifted her hand slightly in a wave.

"Girls are such cowards," said Trave.

"That girl was no coward. Have you ever been swooped down on by such a big bird?"

"No."

"Well, don't speak of what you know nothing about."

Trave felt his cheeks burn, but his opinion remained the same.

They passed the gatekeeper. Trave saluted him. The man bowed deeply and would have spoken, but Trave looked away.

After a while, they passed Umbo's perch on the hill, and then the woods.

Trave turned to look back at Ganet. The setting sun cast an orange glow over the valley and the city walls. The dome of the palace looked small from that distance. For a moment Trave imagined what was going on at home.

Panii would be dozing and snoring. All the servants would be tiptoeing about, trying to make supper without waking him. The stables would be closed up, and the streets would be emptying for the night. If he were there, he would be sitting in the meadow, waiting to be called to supper.

He turned back properly on the horse. The hills leveled out before them, and grassland stretched away for miles. Overhead, Umbo drifted on the currents, never out of sight.

Trave glanced back once more, but Ganet had disappeared behind the little hill they had started down. On every side now he saw only woods and fields and sky. And he was not sorry.

CHAPTER 3
Gris's Camp

It was not altogether dark when Gris stopped for the night, but there was no color in the small light left. Trave could just see the Mahogany Mountains in the distance against a cloudless gray sky.

"Shall we eat?" Gris said.

By now, Trave could think of nothing else. In fact, he could hardly think of anything at all he was so hungry.

"Yes," he said, and plopped down on the ground, waiting.

"Cene first," said Gris.

Trave looked up in disbelief. But the king went on unharnessing his horse, patting the animal as he did. He laid out the tack on a stump nearby and opened a large leather sack filled with grain. This sack he carried over to Cene. He scooped a little hollow out in the soft ground and poured in a measure of grain. Cene fell to immediately.

"Now for us," said the old man.

Trave felt as though he would fall in half if he did not eat soon.

"You may prepare our food or lead Cene down to that small stream when his grain is gone. Which?" Gris stood over him, smiling.

Trave had not planned to do anything but eat and fall asleep. He did not want to walk down to the stream, but he knew nothing about cooking. He was lost for an answer.

"Make a fire before all light is gone," said the king. "I will see to my horse."

The prince stood up and looked around. A few twigs and thick stalks lay about him, and these he gathered slowly. He made a small pile of them. And then it occurred to him that he had never seen a fire started. The fires of the palace were already lit and burning whenever he entered a room.

As he stood in a quandary, Gris returned.

"Oh," said the man, "the flint is in the right flank pouch."

Trave got the flint, but it was no help.

At last he said, "I can't do this."

Gris looked at the boy the way he had looked at the frightened girl in Ganet.

"You don't know how is all."

Gris bent down and sifted through the sticks.

"You have a good start here," he said, "but we need a few dry leaves and a few more twigs."

The king himself got the leaves and sticks and knelt on one knee beside Trave.

"Watch," the king said.

Then he heaped the tiny sticks over a crumpled pile of leaves. After that he struck the flint with a rough metal rod, holding it close to the leaves. A spark flew out into the dusk. He struck again, and many sparks sprang out as the rod rasped over the flint. This time, a leaf caught fire and flamed up suddenly. The fire nibbled at the edges of other leaves, soon catching them up in flame. Atop the leaves, the little twigs began to glow red, and then they too burst with fire.

"Now," said Gris, "we'll add a few sticks at a time, bigger ones each time, until we can lay some large logs on."

Together they fueled the fire; it blazed up boldly as the night closed around them.

Gris brought out a stone dish and some dried meat from his gear. He concocted a hot meat supper in a very short time.

"What is this?" Trave asked.

"Dervin—a kind of stag that lives only in Kapnos."

Trave ate with satisfaction and was overcome with sleepiness almost before he had finished.

"Spread your cloak near the fire and sleep, son."

But Trave could only drop down and half arrange the cloak before he was asleep upon it.

He awoke in the long, damp shadows of early morning. Cene was saddled and the fire was out, covered with a mound of dirt. He put back his cover and realized it was Gris's cloak.

"Gris?"

"Here, son."

The king, reading a book, sat against a stump a little behind Trave. "Good morning."

Trave stood up stiffly. He felt that his legs were weak. He could hear the stream, but he could not remember having heard it the night before. He went down to it and washed.

When he returned, Gris handed him two pieces of fruit.

"What are these?" the boy asked.

"Breakfast."

"Yes, but what are they?"

"Jalalays."

Trave took a small bite of one. A rich, sweet pulp and juice filled his mouth. The best fruits of Gadalla would seem tasteless beside this, he thought. He ate them both quickly and felt as though he had eaten a full meal.

"Where did you get them?"

"In Kapnos. They keep for months. All my soldiers carry them."

"They're delicious."

"Come. The day gets ahead of us."

They rode on toward the Mahogany Mountains and Gris's camp. Trave tried to watch what signals the king gave his horse, but often the horse picked up his pace or changed direction slightly without any word or sign.

"Did you tell Cene to go faster just now?"

"Yes."

"How? I couldn't tell."

"I shifted my weight forward a fraction."

Trave wondered if only Cene responded like that or whether all horses did. He hoped his horse would be obedient.

"Gris," he said. "I haven't seen Umbo!"

Gris pointed ahead and to the left. A small dark dot moved above the mountains.

"Is that him?" Trave could not be sure.

Gris nodded. "He came this morning before you woke. He had a real snake this time."

"He did? Oh, splendid!"

The sun rose high overhead, and Cene paced on. Trave felt hot, and his leg muscles ached. He thought of lunch, but did not mention it.

After what seemed hours to Trave, Gris said, "There is the camp."

Trave squinted and saw a black line along the foot of a mountain. "That black line?"

"Those are the pavilions, Trave."

As they rode on, the black line became poles with canvas tops. Shortly a rider appeared, coming toward the king and Trave. He came at a steady gallop, leaving a trail of dust.

"Tanarad," said Gris. "One of my captains."

The rider slowed as he approached.

"Welcome, Your Grace," he said with an accent.

Gris nodded. "Captain. Ride with us."

"Thank you, sir." The newcomer swung his horse in step with Cene.

"This is Trave, Prince of Gadalla."

"Your Highness," said the captain.

"Tanarad is a Dideran, Trave. But out of respect to your land, he—and all of us—speak Gadallan while still within its borders."

It had never crossed the boy's thoughts that all the world did not speak Gadallan all the time. All the traders spoke Gadallan, although with many accents.

"Thank you," said the prince.

The captain smiled widely, happy to have pleased the prince.

"News?" asked the king.

"A little, sir. A Kolonian came into camp last night. He said there are Sardan soldiers in Ganet."

Gris's mouth made a fine line.

"That is all, Your Grace. I rode out only because I heard you coming, not because the news was urgent."

"Heard?" said Trave, looking at the soldier, amazed.

"Diderans have exceptional hearing. They can hear water under the ground, or flowers opening—or, on still nights, the breathing of their enemies," said Gris.

Trave stared at Tanarad. "Your ears don't look so much better than mine."

Gris and Tanarad laughed and pricked up their horses.

"Diderans are also excellent archers," said Gris. "And fine horsemen."

Trave looked with keener interest at the captain.

"Why do you ride with the Kapnos guard?" asked Trave.

"I have lived in Kapnos since I was a small boy," said the Dideran. "It is my country. Gris is my king."

Trave said no more, but he wondered how someone could leave his own country for another.

They arrived at the camp. It was spacious and well laid out. The soldiers cheered to have their king return. From every tent and pavilion, men raised the hilts of their swords to their brows in salute to Gris. The king waved, calling many by name.

"There is food, sir," said Tanarad.

"The prince is hungry, I'm sure," said Gris, dismounting. "Will you care for Cene?"

"Gladly, my lord," said the captain.

The king entered his tent, and Trave went toward the smell of cooking. He found a wiry, bearded man at a kettle over a fire.

"Hello, young fellow," said the man in a squeaky voice. "Want a little kalu?"

"Is it food?"

"Why, of course, it's food. Where are you from?"

"Gadalla."

"Well, sure. I could have knowed from your talk. No accent."

"Gris has no accent," said the prince.

"No, he don't. But then he's Gris, ain't he?" The wiry man chuckled. "Here—you'll like this."

And, indeed, kalu was much to the prince's liking.

Trave asked, "Are you from Kapnos?"

"Yep. Well, the Northlands, way, way north. Two days above Cordus, the capital."

"What's it like there?"

"Up north? Cold, my boy, but beautiful. The snowy mountains rise straight up out of an ice-blue sea and go right on up to the sky. You ain't never seen such a blue as the sky is there."

The cook shook his head once, smiling to himself. "Ain't nothing like it."

He saw that Trave had finished the kalu. "I'd give you a bit of barray meat, but some white-feathered thief made off with my last ring this morning."

Trave glanced around. "What?"

"A big owl. Swished right in here and took off with a ring of barray."

"Where did he go?" Trave was not sure he wanted to hear the answer.

"Right over there. See, in those trees. I figure, well, he's hungry, too, you know." The cook laughed to himself.

Trave tapped his leg with his hand, thoughtfully.

Tanarad strode up. "The king would like some nadeel to drink, if you please."

"Right away," said the cook. "I'll take it myself."

"And a bit of barray, perhaps?"

"Not likely, captain. I'll explain to the king."

Trave made a little moan.

"Not sick are you, young fellow? I ain't never had nobody get sick on my food."

"It's not the food," said Trave.

———

The camp, for all its order, was an extremely busy place. Every man was employed somehow—polishing harnesses, honing swords, or caring for the horses. Trave searched for a place to sit and watch, but with all the industry around him, he felt somehow that he should be doing something.

He decided to work with Umbo awhile. But when he opened his pouch, a terrible stench rose from it.

"Spoiled," he said, throwing down the pouch.

"What's spoiled?" the cook asked.

"This meat."

Cook picked up the pouch. "Yes, I believe it is. Well, no matter. We'll feed you."

"It's not for me," Trave replied, disgusted. "Princes do not eat bird meat."

"What kind of bird was it? Looks like animal meat to me."

"It is animal meat," said Trave, beginning to lose patience. "I feed it to my bird."

"Oh," said the cook. Then he looked up keenly. "Oh." He grinned. "So he's yours, is he?"

Trave nodded.

"You're a prince, you say?"

Trave nodded again. "I am."

"Well, I could have knowed." But that was all he said. He walked away with the pouch.

"Now see here," said Trave to Umbo when he found him. "You must conduct yourself better. What has gotten into you?"

Umbo cocked his head at the boy and blinked.

"You're making me look bad."

Umbo clicked in his throat.

"You do not have to steal. I will feed you."

The owl lifted one wing to peck under it.

"Listen. Are you listening? Never fly at girls."

Tanarad had stood a short way off, waiting to speak.

"Prince Trave, the king would speak to you."

"I come." He looked once more at Umbo. "Now mind what I say, bird."

Umbo regarded him silently, blinking slowly, as if he would fall asleep.

"What do you name your bird?" Tanarad asked as he and Trave walked toward the king's tent.

"Umbo," said Trave, stiffening a little at being asked a question first. Captains should wait to be spoken to, he thought.

"What does it mean?"

"Shield handle," said Trave.

"Ah, a good name." Tanarad said no more.

"Can you really hear flowers open?" Trave asked.

"Yes."

"What do they sound like when they open?"

Tanarad thought. "Like a whisper in a dream."

"Don't you go mad, hearing everything?"

"I can hear everything, but I don't listen to everything," said the captain.

They arrived before the king.

Gris stood outside his tent. "We leave tomorrow. My men will break camp before day."

Here he unrolled a map and showed it to Trave.

"We are here. By sundown tomorrow we will be over the Saum River and perhaps out of Ogham Pass."

Trave nodded solemnly.

"It is no easy ride," Gris continued. "But I cannot hold back my men for you. So you must ride beside me and do as I say."

Again Trave nodded.

"Good," said Gris, smiling his warm, wide smile. Then he nodded to someone.

A soldier leading three horses came before the king.

"Now," said Gris, "choose a horse for yourself."

Trave had not forgotten that the king had said back in Ganet, 'You may choose a horse at my camp.' But he was still surprised now, for he was not used to promises being kept.

There was a black horse, a brown one, and a spotted one. They all stood alert, their ears forward and eyes bright.

"All fine horses," said the king. "Worthy of a prince."

Trave looked at them wonderingly. He knew little about choosing horses, but there was something about the black one.

"The black one," he said at length.

"A wonderful choice. He is the grandson of a horse your father gave me as a gift."

Trave felt a shiver run over him.

"How will he be called, Trave?" asked the king.

The boy paused. "What did my father call his horse?"

"Lenap."

"Lenap, then," said Trave. "After father's horse."

"Done," said Gris.

Later that afternoon, Tanarad taught Trave to mount and dismount, to sit comfortably, and to carry his feet well in the rings. He made Trave mount again and again, until the prince thought his legs would be jelly.

"Enough," said the Dideran at last. "Tomorrow's ride will be a far better teacher than I am."

Trave willingly gave over the lesson. He walked toward the cook's area.

"The horse first," said Gris, watching from a pavilion.

Trave looked back. "Tanarad has him."

"He is your horse."

"I am a prince."

"So there is no excuse at all. Go."

Trave stood a moment under Gris's gaze, and then trudged wearily back to Lenap.

"I'll show you what to do," said Tanarad quietly.

The prince did as he was shown, but not altogether cheerfully.

At dusk, the entire camp sat down to eat, Gris among his men. There was plentiful food and a rich fruit drink and much talk.

The cook, pleased with his efforts, sat down himself to eat. By and by he came over to Trave and handed him his fowling pouch.

"Put a few scraps in there, for your winged thief, I did. Nothing we'll miss, understand." He grinned a crooked little grin and winked.

Trave took the pouch. "Thank you."

"Why sure, Prince. Just keep him out of my good supplies, and I'll say we is even."

Gris walked among the soldiers. They seemed to wait in groups, even after finishing the meal, for the king to come by. Each looked at Gris directly and answered him distinctly.

The king came around to Trave shortly.

"How was your riding lesson?"

"Well enough," said Trave. He looked up sideways at the king. "I had thought you would teach me."

Gris regarded him closely but said nothing. Trave felt as though he should look away. He knocked his cup against the pole of a pavilion.

When the king spoke again, his voice was low. "There is much you might learn from Tanarad."

Trave felt hot blood creeping up his ears. But he made no answer.

An outrider came running up and saluted Gris.

"Sir, we have taken a spy."

"Bring him."

The outrider stepped back, and two soldiers came forward into the firelight with a man between them.

The spy cocked his chin up defiantly. The light of the fire flashed on his helmet, revealing an open-mouthed iron snake.

Trave recognized the man as the shadowy figure he had seen in the archway back in Ganet.

CHAPTER 4
Out of Gadalla

"What is your name?" demanded Gris.

The fire lit the even features of the stranger. His eyes were dark, like black pebbles under the water. His chin was beardless.

"Thag." He threw out the name as he would throw down his gloves in a challenge.

"So you speak Gadallan. But you are not a Gadallan," said Gris.

The man stamped his iron-soled boot for a reply.

"You are a high-ranking Sardan, are you not?" Gris stood with his arms folded across his chest.

Trave could see that the red leggings the man wore were made of a strange, thick leather of an uneven grain.

When there was no answer, Gris ordered the Sardan held at swordpoint near the fire. Then he and Tanarad walked away to talk.

"Just that one?" said the king.

"He was alone, your grace. I heard no others."

"How close to camp?"

"A spear-shot from the last pavilion."

"Daring, isn't he?" said the king with a little smile.

"Or stupid." Tanarad had a short supply of patience.

"It is some kind of trick," Gris said. "No Sardan of that rank would be caught so easily."

"What shall we do with him?"

Gris looked back toward the prisoner.

"Take him to the first prison in Kolonia. And keep a wary eye in the meantime," he said.

———

Trave slept heavily, never once turning in his sleep. He woke with stiff legs and shoulders. He rubbed his neck and stretched his legs. He stood up slowly, unbending like a rusty hinge.

"A few days of riding will cure you," said Tanarad, passing by.

The camp had disappeared around Trave. Canvases and poles lay neatly packed in wagons; all fires were out and the places made level. All horses except Lenap were saddled and waiting.

"Quick, now, Prince Trave," said the captain, "the king is ready."

Trave managed to harness his horse and climb on with a little effort. He took the heavy reins in his hands as he had seen Gris do, and Lenap moved forward.

The cook trotted by on a brown horse. "Here." He tossed the boy a jalalay. "You missed breakfast."

The prince rode beside Gris as the company rolled forward. He found he had to hold the reins tightly to keep Lenap at a walk.

"Try to use your legs and weight more," said Gris once. "Don't wear out your arms and the horse's mouth."

Trave tried, but he did well just to stay upright in the saddle.

The sun got higher, and the land warmed. Soon it was hot. A lather appeared along Lenap's neck strap. Trave began to wish he might walk awhile, but he knew he could never keep up on foot.

Gris looked over at the boy. The prince's face was beaded with sweat and his shoulders sagged.

"I will stop just after noon," said Gris.

"Don't stop for me," the boy said.

"I'm not," he said, and looked toward the pass with a smile.

They had ridden seven hours when Gris called for a rest. They were well into Ogham Pass.

"How come we've only come this little way?" asked Trave, looking at the map.

"Takes time to move this many men," Gris answered, taking a drink from a silver horn he carried on his saddle. He motioned to the cook, who presently brought Trave a drink.

Trave lifted the cup. His hand shook, and he steadied the cup with his other hand. "We made better time coming to camp on Cene," he said when he had drunk.

"Cene is no ordinary horse. Rest some, son. We will come to the river shortly, and we must all be alert."

In an hour the whole company moved on. Trave resumed his position beside Gris.

Umbo flew in from one of his adventures. He coasted over gracefully.

The Sardan prisoner suddenly bellowed and kicked the horse he was tied to. The animal bolted ahead with a leap, dragging forward the soldier who guarded him. Thag broke away and rode with his hands still tied to the saddle.

One of the captains cut him off, restraining the wildly tossing horse.

"Let go!" Thag roared in his native tongue. "Let go!"

The captain held him fast.

Trave's own horse pranced around in a tight circle. Gris took hold of its bridle.

"Send the owl away," he said to Trave.

Trave looked around in confusion.

"Umbo," he called out, "go back!"

For once Umbo obeyed on the first command. He arced away to the trees.

The Sardan's head fell forward and his body slumped. The horses simmered down.

"What's going on?" Trave wanted to know.

"Sardans," said Gris, "fear owls above all else."

"Owls?" Trave was astonished. "Why?"

"One of their young princes was once snatched away by an owl. Their king then commanded that every owl in the borders of Sarda be killed. There was a great slaughter of the birds, but the giant bird who took the child was not among the kill. However, it returned one night and stood on the chest of the Sardan king as he lay in bed."

"And then?"

"And then they found the little prince, the next morning, safe in a tree not far away."

"Why does that make Sardans afraid of owls?"

"The child told them that the owl had lifted him away from a reen—a creature whose bite is certain death."

"Ah," said Trave. "The owl saved his life! Do the Sardans fear revenge then?"

"They began to worship the owl as a god—but they fear it mortally."

"Is the little prince king now?"

"He was a ruler. But that was a thousand years ago." Gris signaled Cene to move out ahead of Lenap. The two rode on silently.

The mountains now rose up steeply on either side of the pass. A thick stone wall ran along the east side, about as high as the horses' heads.

The wall began abruptly, in the middle of a sheer rock rise.

"We have passed out of Gadalla," Gris called back. "We are now in Kolonia."

"Did the Kolonians put up this wall?"

Gris dropped Cene back to ride by Trave again. "Yes, they built it and chiseled the drawings and writings centuries ago. It stands here to welcome travelers and to make their passage easier."

"What is all this writing?" Trave could not read much of it.

"Stories of kings and craftsmen, of captains and common people—Diderans, Kolonians, Torridians, even Sardans—from ancient times 'til now."

"Splendid!" exclaimed Trave in Gadallan. "Can you read all the writings?"

"Yes."

They passed a section of writing that was chiseled in small, even wedge shapes, line upon line.

"What language is this?" Trave wanted to know.

"Dideran," said the king.

"What does it say?" Trave looked at Gris expectantly.

The king's blue eyes seemed brighter than usual. He glanced over the words.

"It tells of Enna," he said. "A Dideran lady."

"What about her?"

"It's a long poem, telling of her beauty, her bravery, and her kindness."

"Tell me some of it," the prince said eagerly, forgetting for the moment how tired he was.

"It says that she can heal a battle wound or a broken heart, that she knows every creature and plant in her mountain valley home."

"Really? Does it tell of any of her deeds?"

Gris continued. "Here it tells why the Lady Enna is safe from the terrible skreels."

"What are skreels?"

"Giant birds of prey that kill humans."

"Why is she safe?"

"Once a skreel fell, bleeding into the valley among the Brass Mountains where Enna lives. It would have died there, but the lady, knowing the bird would have killed her if it could, healed it anyway. When it climbed the air again, it circled the valley five times. Since then, Enna has walked unharmed among these birds, and, it is said, she has been guarded by them more than once."

Trave could hardly believe one lady could have so much power. "Is all this true?"

"It is." The king's tone rang with certainty.

"Well," said Trave, "she must be very wonderful indeed."

"Indeed," said the king, as if he knew.

Trave rode awhile without speaking. Then he asked the king, "How old are you?"

Gris laughed. "A little older than my beard."

Shortly, from some way off, Trave heard a pounding roar. It got louder and louder.

"What is that?"

"The waterfall where the Saum River comes into the pass. Extraordinarily high and beautiful. The river comes from a thundering fountain on the highest peak up there." Gris pointed toward a distant place that could not be seen from where they were. "Another river—the Dag—runs the other way out of the same fountain."

And the waterfall was beautiful. White water came leaping down the steep mountain, sending forth a fine spray where it crashed to the floor of the pass. Around the river the trees grew thick and tall as far up the mountain as Trave could see. The Saum tarried momentarily in a swirling pool at the foot of the falls and then turned out to rush on in its course to the Malus Sea.

The captains shouted above the roar of the water. The men made swift preparations to cross.

"Get onto one of the barges or in one of the randans. I will take Lenap with me," said Gris.

"I don't need to get in a boat." Trave's eyes flashed.

The king, who had been motioning to some of his soldiers, turned his full attention to Trave.

"One day's ride does not fit you to ford a river on horseback. Now dismount."

"I will not be treated like some girl. I am a prince!"

The soldiers near the king got quiet and looked over at Trave.

Gris neither moved nor raised his voice.

"Get down." The blue of his eyes was like deep, cold water.

Trave could find no means to resist the command. He handed his reins to the king. The soldiers looked at one another and then set the ropes of a barge. Gris led Lenap away without a word.

"Say," said one of the young men, "the king should have thrown you into the river."

Trave wheeled on him. "I am the son of a king and the rightful king of Gadalla!"

"Well, this is not Gadalla, is it?"

Trave marched off, thinking perhaps he would turn back. At least in Ganet he was respected.

"Here!" a voice called. It was the cook. "Prince Trave! Over here! There's room on my barge." The cook motioned him on eagerly.

Trave hesitated.

"We're leaving! Hurry along."

The prince considered a moment more and then flung himself onto the barge. He sat sullenly among the grain bags and the kettles.

"The Kolonians lend all these barges and three-seated randans to Gris—every time. Ain't that something, though? Dozens of them." The cook made a funny snorting sound that served as his laugh.

"It's not so much." Trave intended not to be impressed.

"Oh, now. You're just pouting because the king didn't let you drown yourself. Well, you can get over it—it was the horse he didn't want to lose anyway."

Trave kicked over a kettle.

The cook said "pah" and shrugged his shoulders.

Six young Kolonians came aboard with long poles and paddles to steer the barge. They shoved it away from the bank artfully.

Then all six Kolonian bargers leaned into their poles together and the barge shot ahead.

A randan moved slowly alongside. Thag sat in the middle seat.

"Aren't you the prince?" Thag called over to Trave.

Trave just looked at him.

"Anyone could tell by looking that you have royal blood."

Although he made no answer, the prince was pleased.

"Too bad that the king of Kapnos is getting old and stupid, or he'd see it too."

A soldier behind Thag clapped the Sardan soundly on the shoulder with a paddle. "Keep quiet."

Thag grinned slyly at Trave, raising one eyebrow a little and waggling his head.

Again the Kolonian bargers pumped together; again the barge slid forward.

"Let me try that," said Trave.

The poleman looked at him, puzzled.

The cook said something then, in a foreign tongue, and the poleman answered.

"He says you can stand beside him," said the cook.

Trave steadied himself as he stood and then went over and held on to the pole. It surprised him to feel how strong the current was.

When the Kolonian lifted the pole again, Trave's hands went up as well. He marked the angle of the pole and the smoothness of the motion. Again and again he watched and helped. It seemed natural to him, as though he had done it all his life.

Soon they neared the center of the river where the current was stronger. Three bargers put down their poles and held paddles at an angle in the swirling water. The others continued to pole. All this Trave watched carefully.

He looked back to the bank they had left. The river was full of barges. All along the bank, archers stood guarding the pass and the soldiers as they crossed the river.

Some soldiers came across on their horses; some came across in randans, allowing their horses to swim freely. A few horses rode across on the barges.

Gris came last. He held his sword and scabbard up out of the water with one hand and kept Lenap's reins with the other. Cene moved through the water like a ship.

All in all, the whole crossing was a glorious sight to behold. Trave almost wished the river were wider so that he could watch longer.

The Kolonians shoved on the poles to keep the barge moving straight. It looked easy enough, but the bulging muscles in their arms and chests showed that it was not.

The cook's barge was one of the first to hit the opposite bank. The polemen sprang off and hoisted heavy ropes to secure the flat vessel. The cook started ordering his helpers about, worrying over his kettles

and supplies. Trave got off and stood on the bank a little up the river.

The soldiers and the horses came up out of the river, the water streaming off them. Then on through the pass they went, on into the late afternoon.

Trave rode Lenap, but he fell somewhat behind Gris now, avoiding the king's eye. He noticed near sundown that he had a blister where the reins rubbed between his fingers. He also felt that the inside of his knees had been chafed raw against the saddle, despite his leggings. His back ached a little. Surely, he thought, they would camp soon.

But on the king and his royal guard moved, into the lengthening shadows that fall after sundown, and on until the world was nearly all gray. Tanarad told

Trave which stars they followed, but the prince did not listen well.

At last the pass fanned open onto the wide Kolonian plains. The company swung a little north, stopping just beyond the pass for the night.

Soldiers immediately dismounted. They were setting up tents and pavilions before Trave could kick his boots out of the stirrup rings. The cook began to make giant kettles of stew; outriders, who had gone ahead to build fires, remounted and waited for orders from Gris.

Trave slowly let himself down from Lenap. He had ridden over twelve hours. He had never been so tired in his life. He tied his horse to a tree and pulled his cloak from under the flank strap. It was still a little damp, but he did not care. He did not even want to eat. He threw the cloak down as a bed. He would have dropped down in a dead sleep right then, but Gris drew his horse up beside him.

"The horse first," the king said. "Then eat. Then come to me."

Had Trave not been the son of a king, he might have wept.

He unsaddled his horse, watered and fed it, and threw a blanket over it. Then he took a little stew for himself and realized that he had indeed been hungry.

At last he trudged to Gris's tent. Night had fallen fully. Bright fires wavered among the tents, making the men who sat beside them glow orange and red. Trave stopped and stood silent before the king's tent.

Presently Gris came out and sat by the fire.

"Sit down, Trave."

Trave sat, on the other side, across from Gris.

"You rode well today. You learn quickly."

The prince looked deeply into the flames.

"But," Gris went on, "I brook no disobedience from any in my company."

For a while, the only sounds were the voices of men at other fires and the snapping of their own fire.

"A good leader must first know how to follow, son. If you would find your father's medallion, you must be content to follow me yet awhile."

Gris let the silence work. Then he said, "Your father had his reasons for sending away his medallion. If you will not trust me, trust him."

Trave did not look up.

The king leaned back, his face calm and handsome.

"Tomorrow as we ride, I will teach you some Kolonian. Many peoples speak it; it is the language of statesmen."

"Thank you." Trave's voice was low.

"Now sleep," said the king. "You've earned it today."

The prince stood and at last looked directly at Gris. The old king smiled, but Trave did not.

CHAPTER 5

Earthquake and Aftermath

The next day's ride began at daybreak. Trave rode more easily and began to understand the movements of his horse. He learned a few words in Kolonian. It helped that many of the men around him were speaking the language.

"Horse and saddle," said Gris in Gadallan.

Trave said the words in Kolonian.

"Excellent," said Gris.

"I don't know," said the boy.

The old king laughed. "I meant you did well—not that you should translate the word."

"What is the first duty of a king?" asked Gris in Kolonian.

"To learn what is true," said Trave in Gadallan.

"My liege!" Tanarad had ridden forward suddenly. "I hear a storm—or a breaking under the ground."

The prince looked from Tanarad to the king. The men's faces were serious.

Gris rode on, but he did not speak any more. Trave turned a little in his saddle to look behind. The guard rode easily in four columns, the martingales on the horses clinking lightly, and the leather boots and saddles creaking.

Then, a few minutes later the horses began prancing excitedly, tossing their heads and snorting.

Trave held in his wheeling mount. He looked toward Tanarad. "What is it?"

The captain's horse lunged ahead and trotted in a tight circle. Tanarad brought him around, still listening. Then he looked up at the king, his tone even: "It is not thunder, my lord."

Gris whirled Cene about and stood in his stirrups. "Turn out!" he roared to his men.

The soldiers turned their horses out of the columns, riding away from the main rank.

And then they all heard it, a low rumble from under the land. It seemed to be everywhere beneath them. Frantic horses leaped and plunged, blowing and screaming in terror.

Gris rode back through the dispersing lines. "Away! Away!" he ordered to a few who moved too slowly.

Then the ground started to tremble. It moved under the horses' feet; it shook the tall grasses; it quivered and turned over rocks.

The soldier holding Thag's horse maintained his position, his own horse bucking and kicking.

"Release the prisoner," commanded the king.

The soldier cut Thag's ropes and released the reins. The Sardan galloped away.

And then the rumble became a terrible roar. The whole land shook violently, and great cracks gapped open everywhere. Those who could leaped from solid ground to solid ground over the openings. The earth fell into itself and closed again in seconds, and wide ditches pitched open. Some horses and soldiers fell into the holes, and others were thrown down on hard ground.

The ground beneath Trave's horse remained firm while Trave searched wildly for a clear place to escape to. On his right a horse fell in a cloud of dust, but the rider jumped clear. Lenap reared and plunged, straining at his bit. Trave somehow kept him from bolting.

Then, as suddenly as it had begun, the earthquake stopped. An awful silence came behind the roar. A little loose ground slid down into the cracks, and then all was still. For a few seconds, no one moved—not horses, nor soldiers, nor even the king.

When the calm had lasted several moments, Gris urged his horse forward. Those still mounted and able to collect their horses followed his example.

The captains assembled before Gris. Trave brought his horse into the circle. He looked around him. Tanarad was missing.

Gris took in the whole group with a glance. His gaze was calm, but his tone was urgent.

"Find your companions," said the king, "and rescue the survivors."

The men left straight away, turning their mounts out in several directions.

"Secure your horse," the king said to Trave, "and come on foot with me."

The prince, barely recovered from his fright, did as he was told.

Together they walked along the crest of the main gap in the earth.

"Is any man there?" Gris called out again and again. "Is there any man there?"

"A sword!" said Trave, pointing to a ditch.

Gris leaped into the ditch, throwing back the dirt with his hands. A soldier's head and shoulder appeared. The king pulled him up like a root.

The man coughed and sucked in his breath. He coughed again.

"Are you hurt?" said the king.

The soldier squinted into the sun behind the king's head. "No, sir," he answered.

"Trave, help him out," said Gris.

Further on Gris pulled out a man who did not answer him. "Ah, son," the old king said, as he laid the dead soldier at the edge of a ditch.

The prince came behind in silence. He carried water to the injured and recovered swords and helmets. He tied up horses and moved wagons.

Gris walked on and on. Most of his soldiers were alive. Many of the horses had escaped too. Gris ordered his men to set up camp a little to the north.

Near dusk, Tanarad was found. He lay among a pile of rocks at the far end of the main opening in the earth. Some soldiers carried him to Gris's tent and sent for the king.

"Tanarad," said the king, but he said no other word.

They dressed the captain's cuts and washed his face. The king sat by, waiting. The cook built a fire and boiled a broth over it.

"His arm is broken," said one man.

Gris nodded, motioning for the man to let the captain lie undisturbed for a while.

At last Tanarad opened his eyes.

"So," said Gris, "wake up to eat, will you?"

The captain looked a long time at his king. Then he said quietly, "I cannot hear you, my lord."

Gris leaned forward, his smile gone. "Not at all?"

Tanarad tried to speak but sank again into unconsciousness.

"Set his arm now, while he cannot feel it," said the king. "Tomorrow carry him to the innermost pavilion where the injured soldiers are. Have a man attend him when he wakes. I fear he is deaf from the roar of the earthquake."

"Yes, sir," said a man nearby, and Gris left to look again for fallen soldiers.

By nightfall every man had been accounted for. Two were dead; eleven were injured.

Trave helped feed the horses and care for the ones that had been hurt. Seventeen horses had been lost, counting the one that Thag had ridden away.

The camp was quiet that night—no joking over supper, no boasting among the soldiers. Everyone felt the wonder of his own escape and the loss of those who did not escape.

Gris stood under the outermost pavilion, his arms folded across his chest. He looked out at the stars.

Trave came through the camp, looking for him, to ask why he had let Thag go. But when he saw the king, he went back without speaking.

In the morning, they buried the dead. Gris ordered a marker made for each grave. The prince stayed back from the ceremonies, watching from a tent.

At each grave, the king gave a salute holding his sword hilt to his brow.

Some soldiers played curled silver horns and drums. The music was slow and rich. They played softly and solemnly, until everyone had returned to the camp.

Gris walked through the pavilion where the injured lay. He smiled at them and called them fine men. Assured that they all would be well, the king turned in to his own tent, for he had not slept since the earthquake.

For three days, Gris's company stayed where it was. The injured soldiers and horses mended; men repaired wagons and harnesses and made new gear as they could.

The cook took over Trave's language lessons. Mostly the lessons were strings of vocabulary words, many having to do with food, but Trave applied himself and learned them all.

Umbo returned on the second day. Trave practiced with him a while and gave him scraps. Then the prince rode out on Lenap to get better at subtle commands. The horse sprang along easily under the boy's light weight.

On the third day Trave worked again with his owl and his horse, but he grew impatient to be getting on with his journey.

He trotted Lenap south and east, away from camp, to see if Kolonia were endless plains. In the middle of the afternoon, he stopped to rest and eat a jalalay. He sat longer than he had intended to, and when he rose to leave, the sun was beginning to go down. He mounted and headed Lenap back toward camp.

A moment later Trave saw something moving in the long shadows of a stand of trees. Then a horse and rider appeared. The rider spoke.

"We meet again, Prince of Gadalla." It was Thag.

Trave was startled but did not speak.

"Or perhaps you are more than a prince?"

The prince kept his horse walking on. Thag rode beside him. Trave looked at Thag out of the corner of his eye.

"More than king even," said the Sardan, bringing his horse closer to Trave's.

"What do you mean?" asked Trave.

"Anyone who has an owl at his command is surely more than a king." The Sardan reined his horse into step with Lenap. He smiled sideways at the prince.

"What do you want?" asked Trave.

"The question is what you want. You want to be ruler of Gadalla, do you not?"

"What is that to you?"

"I can help you get your throne."

"I don't need any help." Trave's voice betrayed an interest.

"You think the old king will help you, I suppose," Thag said.

Trave looked directly at Thag.

Thag shook his head and laughed mockingly. "He told you there was a medallion, didn't he?"

"There is a medallion," said Trave. "Gris has said."

"Bah! Fool." Thag dismissed the subject with a wave of his hand. "That is all the story of an old man. He's trying to keep you from your throne with all this useless travel."

Trave looked away, unsure.

"A king," said the Sardan, "must take what is his."

"I need the medallion."

"You need an army."

"But Gris said—"

"The old king is a fool!" The Sardan rose in his stirrups and glowered at Trave. "Old ways are for old men."

For an instant, Trave thought the Sardan's eyes glowed with an eerie brightness. He could not tell whether it was the setting sun or his own imagination that caused Thag to look so.

Thag sat back in his saddle and spoke more calmly.

"If you do not care to be king, it is nothing to me. I had thought you were a mighty man, but perhaps you are just another Panii."

Trave drew Lenap up short. "I am no cheat. I am a king!"

"Prove it then," said Thag, pulling his horse around. "Act like one. My lord Sard will be your ally, give you soldiers and weapons—but you must show you intend to rule strongly, not like some tired old man."

Trave considered his choices.

"What do you say?" said Thag as he drew his reins through his fingers and back again.

"I . . . I don't know." Trave felt as if a door were closing on something he still wanted to see.

"You're heading to Wrycan, aren't you?" Thag said.

Trave nodded.

"In three days I will camp at the Rock Tower southeast of that capital city. If you want to be king—

really the king and not some old man's puppet—you will meet me there."

Thag whirled his horse, the one he had ridden away in the earthquake, and sped south.

Trave watched him a few minutes. It seemed—but Trave could not be sure—that Thag had laughed as he turned away. The prince rode on toward Gris's camp, feeling more of a chill than the coming of night should have brought.

———

Thag rode south and never spared his horse. He arrived at Sarda's capital, Rubrum, in the dead of night and went immediately to Sard, his king.

The castle was dimly lit with tar torches, its great gray stones echoing Thag's heavy steps. Sard, the ruler, sat at an iron table in a small chamber, studying a map in the flickering light. Behind him on the smooth stone wall hung heavy battle axes and spiked iron balls on black chains.

"Master Sard," said Thag from the doorway, his left arm bent up and across to his right shoulder in salute.

"Enter." In the damp, stone room the voice sounded somewhat like an animal's snort. Sard's eyes narrowed as he raised his head, as though unused to the flare of the torches.

Thag stood in the doorway but dropped his salute. "I have met the boy."

"And?"

"I think he may join us."

"Think!" Sard jerked fully around from his map to glare at Thag, his iron stool grating on the stones. "What sort of success is that?" He half stood, poised as if to spring at Thag.

"He will come to Rock Tower as we planned," said the subordinate.

"You had better hope so," said the other. He sat down again. "What of the old king?"

"He is yet the king."

Sard glared at his second in command. "Explain."

"I see no weaknesses in him."

"Before our war council meets, I trust you will think of some weaknesses to report," Sard said, slowly tapping one finger on the iron table.

Thag said, "I understand you, master. I could say he lost control during the earthquake."

"Frame your speech well, and you may live to make another."

Thag changed the subject.

"The boy knows about the medallion."

Sard's fist banged down, and the iron table rang under the blow.

Thag continued, "The old king must be taking him to get it."

"He *knows* where it is! I'm sure of it." Sard's anger flared hotter than the torches. "I have always known the old king was the one to watch."

Sard clenched his teeth and leaned across the table, ramming his knuckles against the corner hinges. "We get that boy by device or by force. I care not. And if he lives or dies, I care not. But the medallion is mine!"

———

Out on the plains Trave had picked up a trot because the sun was going down quickly. He had ridden only a few miles when he saw Gris coming down toward him on Cene. Trave felt his temper rise. When he came abreast of Gris, he said, "You needn't have come after me. I wasn't lost."

"I didn't think you were," said the king. "How was your ride?" he asked in Kolonian.

"Good," answered the prince in the same tongue, and continued. "Will we ride on tomorrow?"

"Yes," said Gris, "in the morning."

They traveled a way in silence; then Trave ventured a question, this time in Gadallan.

"Have you ever seen my father's medallion?"

"Yes."

Again there was a silence. The horses' hooves made a steady rhythm in the open air. The leather gear creaked a little.

"Why did you let the spy go during the earthquake?" Trave asked, an edge in his tone.

Gris regarded the boy a moment before he answered. "It would have been wrong not to give him the same chance to live as any of the others."

"He is your enemy."

"True."

"He was your prisoner."

"True. But that did not give me the right to let him die helplessly," said Gris.

Trave did not answer.

"We were not in a battle, Trave."

"I would not be so—" Trave broke off.

The king looked right at the boy but did not smile.

"There is more to being a king than swinging swords and executing prisoners. Strength is not measured by cruelty."

The prince refused to answer. He looked away to the west, sinking his heels deep in the stirrups.

At camp, the soldiers were eating and talking, and some were laughing quietly together. Gris and Trave rode in together.

"Tanarad," said Gris suddenly. "Good evening."

Tanarad had walked out to meet Trave and the king. "Good evening."

"Can you hear us speak?" asked the prince. He was surprised to see the captain, who had not been up since the earthquake.

The Dideran walked with a limp and wore a sling. "A little," he said. "If you are close enough. If I can see your face."

Trave and Gris dismounted.

"Sir," said Tanarad to Gris. "I am unable to guard the camp as I have done. I request that you post me some way out from the center pavilions. Perhaps I can hear if I am away from the camp noise."

"I have already ordered men to take up watch tonight, captain."

Tanarad nodded, looking down. "I'm sorry, sir."

"No cause, son," said Gris. "Retire to the tent. You are of more service to me rested."

The captain saluted and turned away.

"Captain," said Gris.

Tanarad turned back.

"It took six men to replace you."

The captain looked with humble gratitude at his king and then, bowing deeply, left.

Trave and Gris took care of their horses, then made their way to the center of the camp. Gris spoke to his men, loudly, clearly, over the leaping fires and the evening noises of the plain.

"Tomorrow we move on to Wrycan. Steady and paced. No hurry—the council of Kolonia will surely be delayed because of the earthquake."

The men listened and nodded.

"Let the injured horses walk as they will, and we will pace ourselves by them."

Trave felt weary all over at the words. "We'll never get there," he said to the cook.

"Oh, lands," said the wiry man. "Two, two and a half days, we'll be there."

To the prince, two days might as well have been two years. He had no idea how far it was to Kapnos, but at such a pace he was sure he would be as old as Gris when he got there.

"What happens at Wrycan?"

"A council of Allies," said the cook.

"How long will that take?"

"A few days."

Trave threw his plate down and walked off.

The cook said "pah" and frowned.

Trave went out and whistled for Umbo, who did not come.

CHAPTER 6
Sarda

Far to the south the morning rose heavy and hot over Rubrum. An orange sun beat on the sand, and the rays wavered back upward from it like colorless smoke.

Such heat did not penetrate Sard's castle, however. It was still cold and damp in the innermost chambers.

The ruler of Sarda stood alone in the armory of his stone fortress, studying his weapons. There were hundreds—some taken in battles, some stolen, some made by Sardan smiths in their huge forges. He took down an arrow, long and sleek, and even in the dim chamber, its point glimmered like a diamond. Sard fingered the point lightly and smiled.

A voice from the door interrupted: "Master Sard."

The ruler half-turned. "What is it?" he demanded.

The soldier stepped forward, throwing his arm across his chest in salute. "The council is waiting, Master."

Sard nodded once and waved his hand to dismiss the guard. He glanced around his armory once more and then, still carrying the arrow, strode away.

When Sard entered the council hall, the members all dropped to one knee and saluted him in the Sardan manner. Behind the visors of thick helmets, their eyes glimmered. Heads ducked, they glanced at one another, but they did not turn their heads. Sard took his position at the head of the hall and said, after a short pause, "Rise."

Thag was first to speak: "I wish to address the council."

"Make your report," said Sard.

Thag turned to the eleven other members. "I have been among the troops of Kapnos."

A murmur of surprise ran through the hall.

"And," he went on, "I have seen the King of Kapnos for what he is."

Thag looked back at Sard, who nodded.

"Well," said a warrior in thick leggings and the iron boots of Sarda, "what is he?"

"An old man who is about to lose command."

A tumult of voices broke forth.

"How do you know?" one soldier's voice rose over the clamor.

"Because," said Thag, "I was taken as a spy, and yet here I stand."

There was a gasp of admiration for Thag. Sard, displeased, threw out his gloved hand. "Explain!"

"I escaped in an earthquake," said Thag. "The king could hardly control his horse—much less his men."

The Sardan warriors whipped out their swords in salute to Thag, pointing them upward as they cheered.

Sard sprang forward, glowering. "It is not much to escape from such a king, is it?"

The hall fell silent, and the swords were returned to the sheaths.

"There is more important business," the ruler went on. "There is Gadalla. Gadalla must not side with Kapnos!" He spat out the last sentence with such angry force that several warriors stepped back. Sard began to tap the palm of his hand with the arrow he had carried into the hall. His yellow tunic stood out against the stone wall behind him, and the open-mouthed serpent of iron on his helmet seemed to stare at the warriors before him. He went on, more controlled.

"The Prince of Gadalla travels with the royal guard of Kapnos."

A warrior called out, "Let's strike now, while the Kapnos ruler is weak, and the prince is away."

Sard smiled, a small, mocking smile with just the left side of his mouth. His face had an evenness of feature that seemed out of keeping with his angry nature.

"We will convince the boy to join us," he said. "To get him, you will treat him like a king."

"Why not take what we want?" said another, older warrior. "Surely we can take the weakling Panii."

"So," said Sard, "you would all run headlong into another war. How soon you forget your defeat." He scanned the room slowly, looking for any challengers. "Gadallans are no fools at war—or can you not remember how they cut down your front lines and drove you right through Rubrum to the Malus Sea?"

He paused, but no one spoke.

"We will take Gadalla as I say. If the boy is with us—we rule Gadalla and pay nothing for it."

There was no resistance in the men. Only Thag's eyes remained hard, and his chin was set.

"Do as I command," said Sard, "or I will get officers who do. Now get out."

The black-clad company dropped to their knees, saluted Sard, and backed out of the hall, their iron soles clanking on the stones.

"Thag, remain behind," said Sard, and the warrior stopped.

The rest of the council disappeared through the heavy doors and pulled them shut. The clang echoed and died away.

"I have decided," said Sard, "to meet the prince at Rock Tower myself."

Thag's hand, which rested on the hilt of his sword, closed tighter slowly. His mouth made a thin line, but he said nothing.

"He must not be allowed to side with Kapnos." Sard's eyes narrowed. "I mean to rule Gadalla."

Thag nodded once. "Yes, Master Sard."

"Bring half my royal guard to Skreel Forest in four days."

"But the skreels—"

"Coward. We will get out before they return at noon."

"But why that—"

"Silence! I chose the forest because it would be a rare uplander that could follow us there." Sard arched his eyebrow cunningly. "Only Gris, the old King of Kapnos." And then he laughed a cold laugh.

"Even so—"

"Even so," said Sard, "I want the boy—before he gets the medallion. He would trust the old man too much by then. And when the old king comes after him—well, what match will he be against my soldiers in that black forest?"

Thag prepared to speak, but did not.

"Then," said Sard. "I will have it all—the prince, the medallion, and Gris, the vile king who tried to ruin me." He smiled at the thought. He nodded for Thag to leave.

Thag did not move.

"Well?" said Sard.

"I think we should take Gadalla now."

Sard snorted. "Is that what you think?" He strode toward a pillar and then wheeled back on Thag. "What will you do with the war council at Wrycan? With the King of Kapnos one hard day's ride from Gadalla's borders? Or do you believe your own lies about the King of Kapnos?"

"Your pardon, Ruler," said Thag, "but the King of Kapnos travels with only his royal guard—not an army."

"And what will you do with the standing army of Kolonia?"

"Kolonians are hardly to be considered soldiers, Your Grace."

"And what," continued the ruler, holding up the arrow he had carried into the hall, "of the Diderans, those savages that shoot men in the dark by listening to them breathe?"

Sard's voice rang through the chamber.

Finally Thag said, "There will be only a few Diderans at Wrycan, Ruler."

"How many did it take to put this arrow in your last king's heart?"

Thag looked down, his jaw muscles working angrily.

The leader of Sarda walked forward and put the tip of the arrow against Thag's chest. "You are a fool. An idiot. You forget how well I know Gadallan ways. And you forget, I suppose, how weak this army was before I came to power? I had the wits to take this country, and I have the wits to get Gadalla. And do you forget the Gadallan soldiers who wait every night to rally to their king? I will make them rally to *me!* And then I will crush them."

Thag raised his eyes from the arrow to Sard.

"Is there any more you have to say?" asked the ruler.

"No, Lord Sard," said the other, his hand tight on the hilt of his sword.

"Good. Now I suggest you follow my orders. Disobedience is costly." Sard slowly drew the arrow back, smiling with the left side of his mouth.

Thag saluted his leader, swiftly, and left the hall.

Sard, tapping his thick glove with the Dideran arrow, watched him leave.

Chapter 7
The Raiders of Ashenland

Sometime in the night, when the late sounds of the plains had ceased and the morning sounds had not yet begun, Trave woke up. He listened, but he heard nothing. The stars, yellow and white, wavered high over him. The fires around were low and steady. He turned over, briefly considering getting under a pavilion. But he did not want to sleep with the common soldiers. He wriggled, trying to find a comfortable spot for his shoulder, and fell asleep again.

His dream rose up around him then, and he tossed fitfully. He saw himself in Ganet, crowned and robed, riding a great black horse with gold hooves and diamond-studded harness. Around his neck, on a silver and gold chain, hung a round medallion as big as a gold plate. But everything in Ganet was changed. The palace was grown over with ugly, knotted trees, and a thick vine with spiny leaves wrapped itself around the throne. Gris stood nearby, saying, "Cut the vine, Trave. Cut the vine away." But Trave could only stand and watch it grow longer and thicker every second.

He could hear the clamor of his people in the streets. They called to him, "What is it? What is it?"

In a sweat, Trave sat up, awake. All around him soldiers were springing up. Signal horns were blasting. Near him a soldier said, "What is it?" And another answered, "Here comes the king!"

Gris strode between the pavilions. "Turn out," he called. "To your posts. Outland raiders."

He passed Trave. "To the center fires. Go."

Bewildered, the prince made his way through the hurrying soldiers to the fires. Before he had crouched at the inmost fire, all of Gris's men had taken up their positions. Trave felt a little lightheaded, having been rousted from so sound a sleep. He could see, though, that the whole camp was bordered by Gris's soldiers, each with sword drawn and helmet and breastplate on. He spied the cook not far away.

"Cook!" he said in a hoarse whisper.

The wiry man scuttled over on his hands and knees. "Sh-h-h," he said.

Trave did not understand why, after all the noise that had just gone on, he should be quiet. But he obeyed. In a voice scarcely louder than his own breathing, he said, "What's happened?"

"Ashenlanders. Out of Torridia. Terrible raiders."

Trave squinted into the darkness beyond the soldiers. He listened as hard as he could.

"How do you know?"

The cook whispered, "They just raided a border farm north of us. The family escaped. One of our outriders found the family and brought them to Gris."

"Will the Ashenlanders come here?"

"We're pretty far into Kolonia. They usually stay near the border, but when they're on the move, you can't tell."

Trave pondered a moment. "Why don't the border farmers move farther south?"

"Best land in the north. Besides, they won't be run off from what's theirs."

"I never heard of Ashenlanders. Why haven't they raided Gadalla? We have more wealth in any of our cities than all the cities of Kolonia together."

"Pah," said the cook. "A lot you know."

Trave would have said no more, but he was too curious. "Well, why don't they raid Gadalla?"

"For one thing, young prince, they're more interested in meat and grain than in gems. And for another, Gadalla has the Dag River."

"So?"

"Torridians would never cross that river unless they had to."

"Why?"

"Why? Why, because they're afraid of water."

Trave was truly astonished. "Afraid of water! How do they live?"

"We better hush," said the cook. "So the soldiers can hear. Too bad Tanarad had that accident. Couldn't nothing sneak up on us when he was listening."

It did seem to Trave at that moment that it would be well if Tanarad had his hearing back.

The night was completely still around them. No soldier moved; no wind stirred. The fires, low and glowing, did not snap or flare. Now and then, a log that had burned thoroughly and still hung together would let go with a little rush and send up a spray of sparks. Gris walked the circumference of the camp slowly, watchfully, his sword sheathed, his helmet in his hand. Trave watched as long as he could; then his head began to bob a time or two from weariness.

The black of night lightened into the thick gray of earliest morning. At last, Gris was satisfied that all was safe. He nodded to his horsemen, who sounded the dismissal, and the soldiers who had stood like statues for over two hours suddenly came alive. The swish and swack of swords being returned to sheaths and a tumble of voices carried on the cool air.

Trave stood up and stretched. Wondering whether to go back to bed, he looked around to see what the others would do. Most of the soldiers lay down again under pavilions; a few walked about, stretching or talking. He felt awake now, though; so he decided to stay up.

He meandered to the king's tent, thinking he might talk to Gris. But when he came near, he heard Gris talking. Then in the light of a new fire, he saw a Kolonian man and woman, and a boy just a little younger than himself.

The man and Gris spoke earnestly together. The woman leaned against a wagon wheel. She looked very tired, the way the light flickered on her face.

At Trave's approach, the boy looked up. He did not smile, but his eyes were bright with interest. When Trave came no farther forward, the boy stood up and walked toward him.

"Hello, friend," he said in Kolonian. "I am Volar."

He wore the soft-soled, knee-high leather boots of the Kolonian working class. His tightly woven breeches tied at the knee, and his sleeveless linen shirt opened down the front under crisscrossing leather strands. He had sandy hair and dark eyes.

"Who are you?" the lad asked in his friendly tone.

"Trave, Prince of Gadalla." The prince pulled himself up to make plain the difference in their heights.

"Your Highness," said the boy immediately, bowing.

Trave was appeased. "What does *Volar* mean?"

"Palm of the hand," said the other. "A good name for a craftsman." He smiled at Trave.

"I thought you were a—" Trave could not think of the word for *farmer*.

"Farmer?" said Volar in Kolonian.

Trave nodded.

"My father is a farmer. But I will learn harness-making." He looked at the prince to see if Trave had understood. Trave did not appear to understand.

"Leather work," said Volar as he held out the ties of his shirt. "For horses." He looked from the ties to Trave.

"Oh," said the prince, "harness."

"Yes," said Volar. "Good."

"Do you speak Gadallan?"

Volar shook his head. "I'm sorry," he continued, "but you speak Kolonian very well."

Trave felt oddly pleased. "Thank you," he said. "What happened last night?"

The Kolonian boy's face became serious, and he looked away.

"Ashenlanders," he said. His lip curled at the word. "They came with torches and arrows to take our cattle and our grain."

Trave did not understand the words *cattle* and *grain,* but he remembered what the cook had said and guessed what Volar had meant.

"How did you away get?" he asked.

"How did we get away," Volar repeated, politely correcting Trave's Kolonian. "We ran to the stream."

So it was true, Trave thought, a people afraid of water.

"Are all Torridians afraid of water?"

Volar said, "Mostly Ashenlanders, I think." The boy glanced back at his mother. "She is tired. I should go sit with her."

"Wait," said Trave. "What about your—" He groped for the word and found it. "Farm?"

"They took what they wanted and have probably burned it by now."

The boy's calmness, more than his words, shocked Trave. He stood speechless as Volar returned to his mother.

Cook brought the Kolonians something to drink and offered to prepare a meal.

The man said, "No, thank you." He turned back to Gris. "But a little rest."

Gris gave the Kolonians his tent and called Trave to walk with him.

"Gadalla is bordered on the north, as you know, by Torridia. You are cut off from Ashenland by the Dag River and the Mahogany Mountains. Nevertheless, a good king is aware of all potential enemies."

Trave's heart rose at the word *king*.

"Will you go after the Ashenlanders?" he asked Gris.

The king looked down at Trave, but he did not answer. The sun was coming up now, its rays streaming out in all directions. The clucking and chirping of plains' birds grew louder and fuller. Gris watched the sun lift slowly higher and finally clear the horizon.

"Trave," he said, "no king can measure out justice everywhere at once. Would it be better for Volar and his family if we took the one band of Ashenlanders and then let all of Kolonia fall to the Dark Alliance?"

"No," said the prince.

"Well then," said Gris, and he left the prince to answer his own question.

———

Two hours after full sunup, the king ordered the men to break camp, and travel began again.

The Kolonian family rode in the cook's wagon. Trave rode Lenap in Gris's company for some time, and then dropped back alongside the wagon to talk to Volar.

"This is the Prince of Gadalla," Volar said to his parents.

They both said, "Good day, Your Highness."

Trave nodded and rode on a moment without saying anything. Then he asked, "Will you learn to make harnesses in Wrycan?"

"Perhaps now," said Volar, looking to his father. But the man shook his head as if to say he did not know.

Trave felt as if he had opened a window before the rain had stopped. He brought up a new topic.

"Would you like to see my owl?"

"An owl! Yes, let's see him!" Volar's open friendliness disarmed the prince every time. He found himself grinning in a most common way.

He whistled high and long. They waited. He whistled again. They waited. He whistled a third time.

"Perhaps," said Volar politely, "he is out hunting."

"He should come anyway," Trave said, a little hotly.

And then Umbo came up behind them, casting his shadow over them as he passed.

"Oh," said Volar, "he is a handsome one!" He shaded his eyes to watch Umbo. "How is he called?"

"Umbo."

"What does it mean?"

"Shield handle."

"Ah, a good name it is." Volar looked back to Trave. "We do not have owls in northern Kolonia. But we have weelans."

"Weelans?"

"Yes. They look much like owls, but they are sleeker, with longer feathers. It is said they build their nests from gold wires that they spin themselves."

"Really?" Trave's eyes widened.

"So it is said. I have never seen a weelan nest."

"Do you believe what is said?"

"I do not disbelieve it."

Trave rode a little forward of the wagon to talk with the cook.

"Why are Ashenlanders afraid of water?" He spoke Gadallan.

"Can't say as I know," said the cook. "Maybe because they get so little of it. Fear of the unknown, you know." He laughed his laugh.

"What do they look like?"

"Ah. Ugly fiends. And dirty, too, as you can imagine."

"How come there is good farmland on the Kolonian side and desert on the Torridian side?"

"Because Kolonia is lower and all the little streams roll down out of the mountains and right across her."

"Does it never rain in Ashenland?"

"Never."

"How can the Ashenlanders live without water?"

"They can live without it because they don't need it. Now don't be a-botherin' me with no more questions."

Trave smiled. Perhaps, he thought, he had drained the cook of information.

Umbo chose that moment to make a perch on the back of the wagon seat. He clicked loudly at the cook, who looked out of the corner of his eye at the bird.

"Nor you, either, you winged thief."

Umbo seemed to understand the insult, for he fluttered and flapped violently for a moment and rose off the seat. Then with deliberate purpose, he landed squarely on the cook's head.

"Umbo!" said Trave, but his stern intent was lost in laughter.

"What's this?" the cook said, trying to duck away and swinging his arms up.

Umbo maintained his balance, apparently content with his new perch.

"Get off, you cousin to a buzzard!" The cook was standing now, but keeping his horses in.

Trave laughed so hard that he had to lean forward to stay in the saddle. Volar laughed as hard as Trave. And Volar's father laughed, and even his mother, who had not even smiled before that, laughed a little.

Word passed along until it reached the king. Gris turned round in his saddle to see. He laughed aloud.

The cook gave over the fight and sat down glumly. Umbo calmly stretched out his wings to steady himself.

"Owl soup, one of these days," the cook muttered to Umbo. "Owl soup, mind you."

But Umbo only clicked in his throat and looked toward Wrycan.

CHAPTER 8
Decisions at Wrycan

Early on the third day after the earthquake, Gris's company rode into Wrycan. Thick gray clouds had rolled in overnight, and a white mist fell across the land, beading the faces of the men and horses as they came.

Trave sat his horse well. He carried his heels low and held the reins less tightly than he had. Around him jingled the trappings of the soldiers' horses. His own saddle creaked as he shifted his weight.

The gates of Wrycan swung wide for them, and in they rode, steadily, quietly. Gris nodded to the gatekeepers who called out to him, "Live long and well!"

Just past the entrance, a group of men in purple and white on tall black horses waited to salute the king and his companions. Gris urged Cene ahead, and the foremost rider of the Kolonian group rode forward.

The two men grasped right arms, in the manner of kings.

"The Governor of Kolonia," said a soldier to Trave.

The governor had a young face and clear, bright eyes. His purple cape fanned out over his saddle and the rump of his horse. He and Gris rode on side by side.

The rest of the Kolonian company fell in behind the leaders. Kolonians and all rode on toward the large pillared building in the center of Wrycan. The earthquake had not shaken the capital city.

Even though the mist was heavy, Kolonian tradesmen stood along the street, waving and calling out to their governor and Gris, who both waved back.

Trave wished he were riding with the kings. He looked over at Tanarad beside him. The captain rode straight and well despite his injuries, but Trave still thought himself better than his company. Tanarad did not talk much because it was impossible for him to hear Trave's words over the noises of the horses and the gear.

The king and all who rode with him were led to a splendid banquet. Long tables, heavy with platters of meat and silver pitchers, ran along three walls of a great room. In the center were many smaller tables with tufted, beautifully carved stools around them. At each table were twelve gold plates, hammered to a wonderful thinness. Around the rim of each plate were raised figures of horses and men, of buildings and trees, and of ladies and flowers, all telling some ancient tale of Kolonia.

Trave filled his plate with thick slabs of meat and three thick pieces of a heavy bread covered with a sweet, sticky sauce. A lady dressed in blue and silver poured him a drink that was at once both tangy and sweet, and Trave sat down with pleasure to eat. The Diderans, he learned from a soldier at his table, had provided the meat. It had a strong, wild flavor.

"What kind is it?" the prince asked.

"Taruda. A stag from the northern end of the Brass Mountains."

When all the soldiers were seated, the governor and his wife sat down with Gris at the center table. The governor's wife wore a deep purple gown, drawn in at the waist with a gold chain. The ends of the gold chain hung nearly to the floor, each ending in a little gold and silver lily. The lady's thick golden hair, braided and wrapped around and around her head, made such a crown, as Trave thought, that she would never need another.

For a moment, he remembered the golden braided hair of the girl who was on the steps in Ganet and wondered, briefly, if she ever wound her braids around her head.

Presently, musicians entered, playing a quiet tune on wooden instruments. The instruments, shaped like hunting bows, were strung from upper to lower curve with wires of a light, springy metal that Kolonian craftsmen could pull as fine as thread. The musicians wove among the tables, playing all the while, until their music fell evenly on every hearer. Tanarad watched the players—a little sadly, Trave thought.

"Is Tanarad a musician?" he asked one of Gris's men.

"He used to play a Dideran flute sometimes, sir," the man answered. "We could never hear it; the notes were so high and fine." He paused. "He probably couldn't hear it now, either."

"What sort of instruments are played at Gadallan feasts, Prince Trave?" asked one of the soldiers at Trave's table.

Trave looked up blankly. He did not know. He had never been at one of Panii's banquets, and he could not remember having heard music at the palace.

He was spared having to answer by a girl in blue who had come to his table.

"Are you Trave of Gadalla?" she asked in Gadallan.

"I am," he said, surprised to hear his own language.

"The King of Kapnos would have you join him at his table, sir," she said.

Trave rose and took his plate to the king's table, where he was seated beside the governor's wife. She was saying something to her husband.

The governor's wife had a laugh like many little bells ringing together. Trave supposed it was always like early morning wherever she was.

"Welcome, Prince Trave," she said in Gadallan.

"Thank you, Your Grace," he replied, and could not by any means understand why he blushed.

"Have you been away from home long?" asked the governor.

"Not long," said Trave in Kolonian, and Gris smiled.

"Ah!" said the governor and his lady together, pleased.

"You learn quickly then," said the governor. "Who is your teacher?"

"The king," said Trave, "and nearly everyone here." He looked around him at the soldiers.

"A fit answer," said the governor, more to Gris than to Trave.

Gris nodded but said nothing.

"Have your travels been exciting?" the lady asked Trave.

"At times, Your Grace," he said, stealing another glance at her hair. "We crossed the Saum and then there was the earthquake. And the Ashenlanders."

"Yes," said the governor. "Gris has told us of the Ashenlanders."

"What will happen to Volar?" Trave asked.

"Volar?" asked the governor.

"The Kolonian boy," said Gris.

"Ah, of course. The boy and his family are under my roof for now. They are free to stay in Wrycan or go back to their farm."

"But Volar wants to learn to make harnesses," said Trave.

The lady looked pleased, but Trave could not tell what he had said that pleased her.

"Then I will see that he learns," said the governor, smiling.

A Kolonian general came up to request a song from the governor's wife. She laughed lightly and rose to much glad applause. She said something to the musicians, and they began to play another tune. She stood beside her husband, her hand on his shoulder, and sang of olden days, of winter, and of kings. The hall fell silent around her.

A goodly king went out to war
In winter, frozen winter.
He stood alone on the kingdom shore
In winter, frozen winter.

The tune was high and lovely. The lady sang it softly. Trave did not know all the words, but he felt them.

To serve his land was all his mind
In winter, frozen winter.
He sailed away on the heaving brine
In winter, frozen winter.

He left his kinsmen, left his wife
In winter, frozen winter,
To guard his kingdom with his life
In winter, frozen winter.

Alone he faced the wicked king
In winter, frozen winter.
And home he came again in spring
After winter, frozen winter.

The governor kissed her hand, and everyone applauded her. After a while she sang again, and when the meal was done, they all left the hall.

It was hours until the council was to begin. Trave walked about the city of Wrycan. The air was still full of mist, as if the weather could not decide if it would rain or be fog. The prince wandered among the shops, looking at the famed craftsmen of Kolonia.

There were barrel makers, wheelwrights, smiths of every kind, weavers, and carpenters. Gadalla needs more craftsmen, he thought. And music, he added after a moment.

When the council met, Trave had a seat beside Gris.

Outside the wide council chamber of Wrycan, green and blue banners shimmered in the light breeze and the mist. Inside, fires burned at both ends of the room to drive off the dampness, and handsome young men stood along the sides holding the flags of Dider, of Kapnos, and of Kolonia.

"Where is my flag?" asked Trave.

"Gadalla is not allied with us," said Gris, simply.

There was a blast of horns, and the governor of Kolonia came in. All in attendance stood and saluted, saying in Kolonian, "Live long and well." The governor returned the salute, and the meeting began.

"Welcome to all," the governor said. "Gris, the king of Kapnos and his royal guard; the commanders from Dider—"

He went on, but Trave whispered to Gris, "Where is the Dideran king?"

"Dider has no king. It is a federation."

"A what?"

Gris shook his head, turning his attention back to the speaker.

"We do not forget the lessons of history," he was saying. "We meet in peace to seek peace."

Trave noticed that his boots were muddy. He tried to work some dirt loose from one boot with the toe of his other.

"I call upon the King of Kapnos, then," the Kolonian said, "the greatest warrior among us and, yet, our best guide to peace."

Trave understood much of what was said. He looked over as Gris rose, wondering what deeds of war the old man had done.

Gris stood squarely, the firelight flickering from the silver on his clothes, his white hair shining. There were a few lines around his eyes, but his cheeks had the ruddiness of a young man.

"Five years ago," he said, and the voice that had filled the court at Gadalla now filled the hall at Wrycan, "we all knew what it was to live in a state of war. We learned the price of holding our borders."

Many nodded solemnly. Trave's interest stirred. He forgot to kick at the mud on his boots.

"Captains of Kolonia, commanders of Dider, the King of Gadalla, and many fine men of Kapnos died in that war."

Trave's heart grew at once proud and sad at the mention of his father. Several men in the hall nodded again.

"To our keeping they left peace and a noble heritage. We cannot lose now what they have passed to us at such great cost."

"Agreed," many said together.

"Say on," said the governor.

"I believe the Sardans are preparing for war," said Gris. "Their object is Gadalla. And after Gadalla, I fear, Kolonia."

There was a great silence in the room.

At last the Kolonian governor asked, "What says the King of Gadalla?"

"He says Gadalla is for Gadalla."

A loud murmur ran through the crowd, as many turned to speak with those beside them.

"Nevertheless," said the king, "the present king is not the true king."

He did not look at Trave, but the prince felt as though he had.

"If we protect Gadalla until the true king takes command, we may avoid another war."

A Dideran commander spoke out, "Sir, will the new king side with us?"

"I hope," said Gris, "that he will be such a king as Dokos was."

Trave's face flushed, although none in the hall, save the governor and those who had traveled with Gris, knew who he was.

"And if he does not, Honored Sir?" ask another Dideran.

Gris stood quietly, as if there were some heavy thing he had to pick up and carry a long way. "If he does not," he said at last, "we will at least have had time to prepare."

For some time after that, the groups from each country discussed among themselves what was to be done.

Gris and his men sat still, mostly without speaking.

"What is a federation?" asked Trave in Gadallan.

"You mean Dider?" said Gris.

Trave nodded.

"Dider is a band of six states under one name, but each state runs its own affairs."

"Why is Gadalla so important?"

"It is important to Sarda because it is rich with gems, and because with it, the Dark Alliance can completely surround Kolonia," said the king. "Once the Alliance has the wealth of Gadalla and the skilled craftsmen of Kolonia under its control, it will be almost impossible to defeat."

Trave thought it wonderful that his country was the object of everyone's interest.

"Why didn't you tell the company here that I am the true King of Gadalla?" said Trave, coming finally to what he really wanted to say.

"Because I do not know that you are," said Gris.

Trave leaned quickly forward. "I am!"

"Show me the king's medallion."

"I am the king, and you know it!" Trave's eyes hardened with anger. "I will speak for myself!"

"No, you will not," said Gris.

The prince sprang up, but the large gloved hand of the king grasped his shoulder and forced him down again.

Gris leaned forward, speaking low and directly at Trave. "You cannot rule a country until you can rule yourself. Speak no more until you know whereof you speak."

Trave sat like a stone—his cheeks hot, his eyes straight ahead. He could still feel where Gris had grasped his shoulder, and he hated it.

The council grouped again into one body. The Governor of Kolonia called for a vote.

"Commanders of Dider," he called.

"Dider," said one of the commanders, "chooses to follow Gris, King of Kapnos."

"Elders of Kolonia," said the governor.

"With your permission," said a man in purple, "Kolonia will accept the words of the King of Kapnos."

"It is decided then," said the Kolonian leader. "We will meet again tomorrow to see how best we may defend Gadalla."

The governor stood. The horns sang out again, and all rose to leave the hall.

Outside it had begun to rain steadily.

Trave went to the stables. He did not want to be with Gris, nor did he want to sit in the soldiers' hall. Umbo was perched on a tack rail near Lenap, blinking slowly in the dim light. He watched the prince calmly, perhaps hoping for a bit of meat.

The prince ignored him and sat down on an overturned bucket. He sat staring downward at nothing for several minutes. The rain drummed on the roof, and Lenap snorted from time to time.

It occurred to Trave at that moment that Gris might be using the medallion to keep him doing what Gris wanted. He felt suddenly as he had felt in the council hall when the king had held him in his seat.

There was a little rumble of thunder a long way off.

At last Trave stood up, his jaw set. He saddled his horse, mounted, and called sullenly to Umbo, who hopped from his perch onto Trave's arm. The little company went out into the rain.

From the portico of the governor's house, Gris watched them. He turned to one of his soldiers nearby. The man came forward, ready.

The king nodded toward Trave, and the soldier bowed slightly to show he understood he should follow the prince.

"Do nothing but watch," said Gris, "unless he calls for help."

The soldier said, "Yes, my lord." He stepped back, bowed slightly again, and left.

Trave stopped near the west gates of the city. He looked around for a tradesman or a market lady. Through an open door at the end of an alley, he saw a blacksmith hammering over a fire. He rode down to him, and called over the pattering of the rain.

"Which way," he began in Kolonian and then halted, not knowing how to say "Rock Tower."

The blacksmith waited, resting his great hammer on the side of the forge.

Trave shrugged Umbo off and the bird flew to the edge of the roof above. The prince dismounted, gathered a few stones, and piled them together in a narrow column.

"Ah," said the man in Kolonian, "which way to Rock Tower?"

Trave said yes, not knowing whether the blacksmith had said "Rock Tower."

"Go south," the man said, pointing, "then east at the first crossroads."

"South," Trave repeated, but the rest he could not follow well.

The blacksmith bent down and drew some lines in the dirt. Trave came in as he pointed out a mark.

"Wrycan," said the man.

Trave nodded, glancing up.

Then the blacksmith drew two lines, one going straight down from Wrycan, the other branching off to the **east** from the first. At the end of the second line, he made another mark and said, "Rock Tower."

Trave stood up, smiling. "Thank you," he said and shook hands with him.

"How far?" asked Trave.

"Two hours," the man replied.

"Good," said Trave.

At the governor's house, Gris had been called back inside. The Kolonians had brought their best musicians to Wrycan to play for the guests. Now they came in with their stringed instruments and bells, making a lilting music as they walked. And after that, there was singing, storytelling, and a feast.

CHAPTER 9

Rock Tower and Beyond

The rain came down harder. Lenap's hooves squished in the mud as he walked along. Water streamed off Trave's head and face, and his cloak, wet and heavy, clung to him. Umbo sat on the prince's arm with his head under his wing.

Trave's arm grew tired after a while. And then it occurred to him that Sardans were afraid of owls, and Umbo became more of a burden than he had seemed even a minute before.

Trave found a thick grove of trees just off the road near the turning he was to make. He shooed the owl into the trees with a warning to stay there. Umbo flew in among the heavy branches willingly, settling out of sight in an old badia tree.

The prince rode on, turning at last at the crossroads as the blacksmith had said.

Rock Tower rose a hundred feet into the air, its brown and white stonework blackened by the rain. It had many narrow windows in its thick round walls and was capped by a pointed metal roof. The dark heavy door was slightly open.

Trave pushed it open cautiously. It swung back on a musty chamber. A small fire burned in the hearth opposite the door. The pelting rain drove the prince inside. He stood, dripping, just past the door, letting his eyes get used to the dimness.

Somewhat left of the hearth, a cloaked figure rose from a wooden bench.

"Trave, King of Gadalla?" The words were Gadallan.

Trave jumped, and a shiver ran over him.

"Who are you?" he asked.

"I am Sard, Master of Sarda."

Trave was indeed surprised. He collected himself. "Where is Thag?"

"It would be bad manners for me," Sard said, coming forward into the dim light, "to send an underling to meet a king."

The firelight showed Sard to be a young man with a straight nose and thin, straight lips. His eyes were dark, and they looked out from a heavy brow, like some animal that did not want to come out of its cave. He carried a helmet in one hand.

Trave closed the door, and the pounding of the rain became a dull roar.

"I have ridden a long way to meet you," Sard went on. "I am honored that you have come."

"Thag says," Trave began, "that you are willing to offer me an army."

"I may be."

"Why?" Trave thought Sard's Gadallan was perfect.

"I want you to be king of Gadalla."

"Why?"

"I'll tell you," said the Sardan ruler. "I do not want the old man to take what is not his."

"You mean Gris?"

Sard flinched as if he had felt a sudden pain in his head. "Yes."

"Why do you not take Gadalla and be king yourself?" Trave asked, dropping his wet cloak to the floor.

"A wise question, Your Highness." Sard swept his hand toward two benches in front of the fireplace, and he and Trave sat down, facing each other. "But I can explain my reasons easily."

Trave sat waiting.

"Sarda is a large kingdom—kingdom enough for me. All I want is to keep it safe. I could take Gadalla with my army; Panii has not the power to rally his army."

A sudden gust of wind blew against the tower. Far away, thunder rumbled.

"But," Sard said, leaning toward Trave, "why should I risk my men when I can get what I want without a fight?"

"Don't you risk them by giving them to me?"

"No, I do not. Your people know you and will accept you as the rightful king. Ride in at the head of an army, and even Panii will bow to you."

The idea appealed to the prince. "But I don't have the medallion."

"Medallion, medallion," said Sard. "What does a king at the head of an army need with such trinkets?"

Trave eyed the ruler evenly. "Is there a medallion?"

Sard hesitated. "No."

"If I accept your help, what will you want from me?"

"I assume," Sard said, "that you, in return, will do certain things for me." He smiled in his peculiar way and turned completely out of the light of the fire.

"What things?"

"You will agree not to make war on Sarda."

"And?"

"And," said the Sardan, "you will not allow Kapnos free trade in your country."

These seemed easy things to Trave.

"What about Gris?" the prince asked.

Again Sard's head jerked as if with pain. "What about him?"

"If he wants to rule Gadalla, as you say, he may ride against me when I am king."

"He would be a fool to come against both of us."

Trave smiled.

"Besides," the ruler said, turning back and tossing a little stick into the fire, "he is too old to do battle anymore." His eyes glimmered with more than reflected firelight.

There was a long pause. The snapping of the fire could barely be heard above the whipping rain.

At last Sard said, "What is your answer, Noble Highness? Shall we work together to get what we both want?"

Trave looked up. There was a flash of lightning, and for a moment Trave imagined that Sard was sneering. But the lightning passed and so did the thought. He put forth his hand. "We shall."

Gris's man, under a badia tree nearby, stood obedient to his lord, waiting for Trave to come out. A sudden burst of lightning lit up Rock Tower and everything around it. Then the feeble light of evening fell round the tower again, but dimmer now, and dying.

Trave and Sard, throwing their cloaks over their heads and shoulders, came out of the tower. The soldier under the tree took a step forward, squinting to see better. Sard saluted Trave in the Sardan fashion.

Instantly Gris's man grasped the hilt of his sword, every muscle tight.

Trave bowed to Sard slightly and mounted his horse.

The soldier, seeing that Trave traveled on willingly, led his horse slowly back into the trees, mounted, and rode straight to Wrycan.

Trave waited, expecting Sard to bring around a horse. Instead, the Sardan drew out a short, curved horn and gave two loud blasts upon it.

Even over the heavy rain, Trave could hear something coming through the trees. Lenap began to prance in place and snort. Trave reined him in, searching the trees for the cause of the sound.

And then it appeared: an immense brown lizard, three times as large as a horse.

Lenap bucked and backed away. Trave held him, all the while staring at the huge Sardan beast.

It made a whistling sound as it came. Its black nostrils flared open and clamped shut rhythmically. The small, dull eyes never blinked. From the top of its head to the end of its tail ran a row of wedge-shaped scales. The tail seemed short to Trave, and then he saw that it had been cut short. A large iron ring, like a giant earring, hung at the blunted end.

The lizard stopped, its head drooping in the rain. Lenap yet danced about, but not in panic.

"Sardans ride grelds," Sard roared. "Follow me to Skreel Forest and see half an army of them!"

He grabbed the iron ring in one hand and pulled the curved tail along as he climbed up the scales to a wooden platform that served as a saddle. It looked like a chair with leg guards to keep the rider from falling out. He took up a stiff whip and thwacked the side of the lizard's neck; then he pulled the iron ring forward. The beast groaned and swung around.

"Come on!" yelled Sard.

Trave followed at a little distance so that his horse would not be afraid.

As near as Trave could tell, they went directly **east**. Darkness fell quickly, and the rain increased. It rained as the prince had never seen it rain, like one huge bucket pouring and pouring water out.

By and by he could no longer see the lizard.

"Sard!" he called.

"Here, boy!"

Trave urged Lenap on toward the sound.

"Here!" Sard called again.

In the torrent Trave had trouble knowing where the shouts were coming from.

"Sard?" he called.

A bolt of lightning tore open the sky, and a crack of thunder shook the ground.

Lenap, his neigh almost like a scream, reared on his hind legs. Trave tried to hold on, but his own fright and the wet gear undid him. As he fell into the deep mud, he caught hold of a fallen branch. He struggled to stand up.

"Lenap!" He groped frantically in the dark. "Lenap!"

Another burst of lightning lit the forest. He saw neither horse nor lizard. The heavy blackness dropped around him again.

"Help!" he called as the rain ran down his face. The storm was so intense that for a moment Trave thought he would drown.

The thunder shook him to himself, and he tried to move forward. The mud sucked at his legs, and the branches tore at his clothes. He slogged on for what seemed to him hours, calling out now and then for Sard and for Lenap. And then he fell.

Or maybe he just dropped, suddenly, into thick, sluggish water that had no bottom. He fought with sudden energy, but down he went anyway, down and down and down.

CHAPTER 10

The Old Bogger

Had Trave had time to sort out his thoughts, he might have tried to swim. But he went under so completely and with such swiftness that he barely had time to close his mouth and eyes.

And just as suddenly, he was pushed by a blast of warm air or water—he couldn't tell which—through a rough tunnel. Then he rolled out with a thud onto perfectly dry ground.

Trave lay in a daze, trying to remember. Nothing seemed to hurt. He opened his eyes.

He was in a cave it seemed, but a well-lit one. From iron brackets all along a wall candles burned brightly. A rock wall arched over him into a ceiling and down into another wall, also studded with candles. It was smooth, clean rock, with no moss or water on it.

Somewhere nearby a voice said,

"What ahoy?

A muddy boy!"

Trave sat up and looked about. Far to the right stood a rumpled little man. He ambled forward on bowed legs, tipping from side to side as he did. He had bright green eyes and yellow hair that flew out from his head in all directions. He was not all that wrinkled, but somehow Trave had the impression that the man was very, very old.

"Did you land here
From far or near?"

The prince said, "Far." Then he added, "Well, near, too."

"Well, I declare!
You don't know where?"

"I am from Gadalla. But I think I came here from Kolonia." Suddenly he realized he was hearing his own language. "You speak Gadallan!"

"So I do—
All others too."

"Who are you?" asked Trave.

"My name is Nog.
I live in this bog."

"Do you always speak in rhyme?" asked the prince.

"I speak in rhyme
All the time."

"Where am I?" Trave wanted to know.

"Here with me.
Can't you see?"

"Then where are we?" Trave smiled at his own rhyme.

"Under Blee Bog

In the home of Nog."

Nog did not seem impressed that Trave had made a rhyme. He shuffled closer to the prince, leaning over to peer at him.

"You're covered with dirt,

But you don't seem hurt."

Trave was up now, trying to scrape some of the mud from his boots. He discovered that his tunic was torn in two places. "How can I get back to Kolonia?"

"I don't know

That I'll let you go."

The prince was taller than Nog, but the words still made him uneasy. "I was with Gris of Kapnos to begin with, but I was traveling with Sard when I fell in here."

The old bogger jumped back.

"I can tell you this:

After being with Gris,

Travel with Sard

Will be very hard."

Trave was surprised. "You know them?"

"Maybe I do.

What's that to you?"

"I am Trave, Prince of Gadalla—and soon to be king." Trave waited for the shock to hit the bogger.

But the little man continued to stare at him, seemingly not amazed that here was indeed a prince, even a king.

"I will rule Gadalla," Trave said, again.

"Who cares,

Red hairs?"

"How dare you speak to me like that? I am a prince!"

"You are a sprig

Who's not as big

As he'd like to think.

Will you have a drink?"

Trave stared at him in astonishment. "No, thank you!" It occurred to him, however, that he was hungry and thirsty.

"Ah, be polite

And have a bite."

The prince was at last convinced to dine with Nog. They had a hard brown bread and a hot drink that tasted like wood smells when it is just cut. The taste was not unpleasant, and the bread was filling.

"Why do you live here?" asked the prince.

The bogger looked at him, mildly irritated.

"Well, soon-to-be-king,

With your solid gold rings,

I've seen everything;

I've been every place—

And all of it's base,

Just an utter disgrace.

I'm tired of prattle;
I'm sick of battle;
I've seen men bleed,
And fall to their greed.
I've just had enough
Of that overland stuff."

The bogger had stood up as he warmed to his subject. Now he returned to his stool.

"Not everything is bad," Trave said.

"Live as long as Nog
And you'll be looking for a bog."

The prince half-smiled and half-sighed. The cave was pleasant, he thought, but he did wonder what Nog did to pass the time. He decided not to ask.

Instead Trave asked the fellow to say rhymes in other languages. Nog did six and then stopped.

"How did you know to speak Gadallan to me?" Trave asked.

"I could tell by your clothes
And the shape of your nose."

"My nose? What about my nose?"

"What about your nose?
Nothing, I suppose.
I just could tell—
(I do this very well)—
By the way it looked,
Straight as straight, nothing hooked,
That you were one
Of Gadalla's sons."

"Oh," said Trave. "How do you tell a Kolonian?"

"All that come from those fair lands

Have strong and careful craftsmen's hands."

"And Sardans?"

The old bogger smiled a little and looked sideways at Trave.

"Until Sardan faces

Are beheld in dark places,

You cannot see

What they really be."

"What does that mean?" Trave asked.

"You have heard

My final word

On the Sardan herd."

"How about men from Kapnos?"

"Enough, enough, I'll take you up.

But first, let's have another cup."

So Trave and Nog drank another cup of the warm, dark drink. Then the funny little man banged against the ceiling with a mallet. Presently a large turtle dropped through the same hole that Trave had come in by.

"Here, Kalop—

Take Trave atop.

And do not stop."

"Which way should I go when I get out?" Trave asked the bogger as he rose to leave.

"I cannot say what you should do.

I must leave that up to you."

"No, no," said Trave. "I mean which way to Skreel Forest?"

"Southwest

Is best."

"Thank you. And thank you for the food."

"One more thing,

Young nearly-king,

For you to know

Before you go."

"And what is that?"

"Good at first

Is often worst.

Good at last

Should be held fast."

Trave looked down at the wild-haired man. "I think you have been in this bog too long."

"Maybe so.

Now off you go.

But hold your breath

Or suffer death."

Nog opened a wooden door on the floor of his cave. Kalop waddled over to it and waited for Trave. The prince climbed onto the shiny square shell, waved good-bye to the bogger, and was gone.

The turtle seemed to go down and then up, first through shallow water and then through deep. Trave held his breath, clinging tightly to the top of Kalop's shell. He felt the water flowing past his ears. His head began to ache from holding his breath. Just when he thought it would burst, Kalop broke the surface of Blee Bog. Trave gasped for air.

"Thank you," he called after the turtle as it dropped back into the depths.

On the shore it was late night, but the stars were out. It was no longer raining. In fact, Trave discovered as he crawled out onto the bank, it had not rained on this side at all.

CHAPTER 11
To Sard's Camp

Back at Wrycan, Gris stood with his arms crossed, listening to the soldier who had followed Trave out to Rock Tower.

"Then I left and rode back here."

The king did not change his expression. He did not move.

"The Sardan leader himself?" he asked.

"As near as I could tell, Your Grace, it was," the soldier answered.

"Thank you."

The young man bowed and left.

For a long time the king stood still, thinking. At last he left his chamber in the governor's house and went to the hall where his men slept. When he entered the hall, his men rose up from their talk and rest to hear what he would say. He spoke to them in the language of Kapnos.

"I must make a journey, perhaps a long one."

No man questioned him.

"Tanarad will be your leader until I return."

Gris turned toward Tanarad and looked several seconds at his sling and bruised face.

"Enjoy the hospitality of Wrycan." He smiled his smile, and many smiled back.

"And when the time requires it," he said, serious again, "defend Kapnos and her friends as only my chosen men can."

Then he smiled again, full and warm upon the whole royal guard. "I am proud to have you in my service."

Then he turned and paced out, motioning to Tanarad as he left.

The rain had slowed down to a steady shower, and the thunder had died away.

The captain and the king walked together on the entrance way.

"How is it with you?" the king turned to look directly at Tanarad.

"I am at your service, sir," the captain said.

"Is your hearing improving?"

Tanarad watched his king's mouth carefully. "No, sir—I can understand words only if I can see the person who is speaking."

Gris stopped walking and looked out at the rain.

"Do you think you are fit to carry on?"

"I do, sir."

"I trust you above all others, Tanarad. You are the most able to lead, even with your injuries."

"Thank you, Your Grace."

"I would order rest for you if duty permitted."

"That is not needed, my lord," said Tanarad, stepping slightly forward. "Rest would not restore my hearing, and my wounds are small and heal quickly."

"As you say," said Gris kindly. "I need you to be as careful and wise in all matters as if you were king. In my absence, you are king."

"I am but a shadow, Your Highness."

"Three things, Tanarad."

"My lord."

"Bring most of our allied forces to the border of Gadalla, from Ogham Pass to Sarda."

Tanarad nodded.

"Leave the best Dideran troops to guard the pass and borders north."

Again the captain nodded.

"Last," said the king, taking a money pouch from his belt, "hire a Kolonian to make a suit of mail and sword for Trave."

"Yes, Your Grace, I will."

"I will also tell the governor of Kolonia all these things. But this last I tell only you."

Tanarad waited in the light of the doorway.

Gris held out his hand, and Tanarad took it, as a son would grasp his father's.

"If I do not return," said Gris, "the Court of Cordus will make you king of Kapnos."

"Sir!" Tanarad said. But before he could make further argument, the old king had slapped the captain's shoulder and was gone into the night.

———

On the bank of Blee Bog, Trave got to his feet. He reached around for his cloak, but it was gone. Wishing he had learned to read the stars, he struck out in what he hoped was a southwest direction.

It was not long at all until he found himself among big, rough trees. The stars immediately vanished. The branches seemed matted together over him.

Trave hesitated. He turned back to the way he had come in—but behind him were only trees, huge trees with jagged bark. He tried walking a few steps in each direction, and then he could not be sure at all which way he had been facing first. Terror all but overtook him, until he remembered that he was the son of a king. So he stood one moment deciding, and then went boldly on as if he knew exactly where he were going.

Deep in Skreel Forest, Thag waited with half the royal guard of Sarda. The grelds they had ridden there were held in a line by an iron chain strung through all their tail rings. The beasts grunted, and roared occasionally.

The trees of the forest stood like grim jailers around the camp, the big limbs locked together like muscled arms. Black leaves, large and flabby, hung matted together as if drenched by rain. Underneath, great lumps of roots had heaved up through the soil and twined around other roots, making the forest floor like a field of boulders.

There were no twitters and scufflings of birds and small animals as in other forests. Here was only the slight smack that a flabby leaf made when it hit the ground.

Many small fires dotted the camp. The light from the fires made a hazy glow in the thick forest. The Sardans stood well back from their fires, just within the light. The language they spoke sounded like snarls.

Thag stood among several of the Sardan warlords, some distance from the center fire.

"What do we need the boy for?" one asked Thag. He spit on the ground.

"Sard says we need him," said Thag.

"Gadalla would fall like a ripe apple," said another.

"If we shook the tree," said Thag, this time pulling his sword out a little to look at it in the flickering light.

"And Kolonia right behind it, now that the old man of the North is too old to protect it," said the first warlord.

"Well, Sard must have his reasons," said Thag in a whining voice. He shoved his sword back in with a thwack.

There was silence around the center fire for a while.

"But if I were Sard," said Thag at last, "I would take Gadalla the warrior's way."

"The Sardan way," said a warlord, whipping out his sword.

"Agreed," said another.

"But Sard says he knows Gadallan ways and will do as he sees fit." Thag threw his hand up and walked away.

"Thag should be our leader. He would have had Gadalla before now. And here we wait in the middle of a forest while Sard runs after some worthless boy," said the first warlord.

"Beware, friend," said another. "Sard still rules."

———

Sard at that moment was still making his way through the heavy forest on his greld. The creature screeched in fright and pain as Sard forced him onward by twisting hard on the iron ring. The greld thrashed through the thick trees wildly. Sard cracked it sharply on the neck to keep it running in the direction of the camp.

Trave, wandering in circles, heard Sard's voice as he shouted to the beast he rode. "Sard!" he hollered. "Sard! Sard!"

At first the ruler did not hear him.

"Sard!" the boy fairly screamed.

The Sardan dropped the iron ring, and the greld stopped.

"Who is there?" Sard called.

"Trave!"

"I thought you drowned!" Sard, who had feared for his own safety, had not turned back in the storm to look for Trave. He had assumed the boy had fallen into the bog. Even now, as Trave had just called out to him, he had been turning over new plans in his mind. He would take Gadalla by force, and perhaps

Gris, whom he expected would follow him in search of Trave.

Trave was so glad to find another person in the forest that he did not wonder why Sard had thought he drowned.

Sard waited for Trave to climb on with him and then pulled up the ring again.

———

Far to the west in Kolonia, the King of Kapnos rode. At the crossroads south of Wrycan, Gris turned toward Rock Tower. From the trees nearby came a rustle of wings and a soft hooting. The king halted Cene. Presently Umbo sailed in through the drizzle, flying close to Gris.

"Very well," said the old king. "Come along."

They passed Rock Tower and traveled east. Umbo stayed close to Gris, perhaps sensing some danger to his master, or perhaps—and this is more likely—he did not want to be left again. Gris rode on, trusting to Cene's steady sense of direction.

Toward morning, he came upon Lenap, winded and head drooping. He got down and stroked Lenap's neck.

"Let's have a look, good fellow," he said. He ran his hand down the horse's shoulders and legs. He looked at his hooves.

"No harm, I see. Shall we travel on?"

It was a clear morning when the horses, the owl, and the king reached Blee Bog. The water was murky and the banks soggy and slick. Gris urged Cene on to pass the south tip of the Bog. And then he stopped, squinting at something farther up the edge.

It was Trave's cloak, caught on a log and trailing into the water. The old king jumped down and pulled it out. He looked around for more signs but found none. He straightened up and looked ahead.

A little farther up was a stone dike the Kolonians had built when Blee Bog had been a lake. Gris walked up to it, turned around, walked seven paces forward, and threw his glove into the bog. It sank out of sight.

In a few minutes, Kalop broke through the dull water, pulling Nog after him. Nog, his yellow hair flattened by the water, stood small and dripping beside the king. He handed over the glove.

"What's this,
Old Gris?"

"Nog," said the king, "where's the boy?"

"Brave Trave?"

Gris waited. Nog answered up:

"Here and gone
Before the dawn."

"Where did he go?" asked Gris.

"How would I know
Where princes go?"

Again Gris waited.

"Skreel Forest he said—

And showed no dread."

"Thank you, Nog."

The bogger grinned.

"An owl and two horses.

Where are your forces?"

Gris remounted Cene. "I thought you knew all the answers."

"Maybe I do—

But don't you, too?"

Gris smiled, amused. "Until we meet again," he said.

"I come to the surface for no other.

Not lady, governor, nor brother."

The king rode away. Nog watched him and then called Kalop to take him under.

———

There was no day in Skreel Forest. The tangled, heavy trees blocked out any light. The fires at Sard's camp burned on. The Sardan soldiers slept.

Sard and Trave rode in on the greld.

CHAPTER 12
What Fire Reveals

Sard dropped the tail ring, and the greld stopped at the edge of the camp.

Thag walked toward them, carrying a tar torch.

"The guard is here, Ruler," he said.

"I see them," said Sard, frowning. "And I have the boy."

Thag bowed deeply. "Prince Trave."

"King, rather," said Sard.

"King Trave," said Thag, bowing again.

Trave nodded once.

"Order the soldiers up. Have food prepared. And take this beast away," Sard said.

Thag dipped his head in the briefest salute. Sard walked away, and Trave followed, a short way back.

When they sat down by a fire, Trave felt how tired he was. But there was no talk of rest from Sard. In fact, there was no talk at all from Sard. He opened the clamps on his iron boots and threw off his cloak.

Trave could see in the wavery, dull light of the fires soldiers scattered throughout the camp. Some were sitting up, but most were sprawled about, sleeping.

Thag came back and handed Trave and Sard iron plates. The prince, sitting closer to the fire than the Sardan, saw that the meat was raw. He put his plate down.

"We will send word," said Sard, tearing at his food, "to the rulers at Trudnar and Brankus that the King of Gadalla rides with us."

"Trudnar and Brankus?" said Trave.

"Capital cities of Torridia and Litoris." Sard threw out the words as if he were speaking to someone stupid. "The other members of the Dark Alliance."

Thag said, "When do we ride, Lord Sard?"

"Now," said Sard, and Trave's heart jumped. "Before the skreels return."

"What about the King of Kapnos?" Thag asked.

"What about him?" Sard glared up at his underlord.

"He will probably be coming after his royal highness here, King Trave."

"Let him come. If the skreels don't get him, I will. I fear him not."

Then Sard dropped his plate and sprang up. "Get those lazy men up, I said!"

Trave sprang up and back at Sard's sudden shouting.

Thag went through the camp, kicking the sleeping men with the toe of his boot.

"Sard is here," he grunted in Sardan. "Get up. Get up!"

Now men gathered, coming among the scattered fires, the thin smoke curling up gray and orange until it disappeared in the matted branches overhead. The soldiers looked like black ghosts outlined in dismal light.

"This is King Trave," said Sard. He reached an open palm toward the boy. He spoke in Sardan now, but Trave knew what was said.

The Sardans put their arms across their chests in salute. Their black boots blended into the shadows so completely that it looked to Trave as if the men rose up out of the damp earth like the dense trees around them.

"He is master of Gadalla, and now our ally. We will ride toward Gadalla tonight. We will take Gadalla without a battle."

A murmur ran over the company. Dropping the salute, the soldiers looked at one another cautiously.

Sard looked hard at them, trying to decide their mood.

"Through Litoris to the Malus Sea and up through Sarda to Ganet."

There was a stir and shuffle, but no man spoke out.

Sard glared at his men, his eyes narrowing. "Do you question me?" he demanded.

Thag's voice rang out: "No, mighty Sard. Hail Sard! Hail Sard!"

"Hail Sard!" cried a warlord, and the chant spread throughout the camp. The shouting began to sound to Trave like the beating of a drum. His heart banged away inside him. His arms and legs felt shaky, from hunger, he thought. He faded back to the edge of camp, but the chant still jarred him. It began to sound like barking.

From where he stood, Trave could see Sard and Thag and several warlords before the main fire. As he watched them, it seemed to him that their faces changed, grew darker, coarser.

He shook his head as if to make the harsh voices and the dismal fires disappear.

Sard let the chant go on for some time. At last he raised his hands for it to stop. It stopped instantly.

"I need two messengers," he said, "to ride to Brankus and Trudnar."

Two soldiers leaped forward, bowing at his feet.

"Come with me," he said to them. The three Sardans walked out toward the grelds to speak together.

The rest of the soldiers waited impatiently by their fires. Thag still stood where he had been standing, watching Sard.

Trave wanted to eat, but he could not find anyone who might be the cook. He wandered a little, hoping to see something he might eat. Sardans spoke to one another in their snarling language and threw their arms about as they spoke.

Trave found a fire that no one stood near and lay down on the lumpy roots underneath the trees to sleep. He missed his cloak now; he curled up against the dampness.

Sard came back from speaking to his messengers. "Where's the boy?" he said to Thag.

"Here somewhere," said Thag, looking about the camp.

"Where?" Sard's voice was hard. His eyes glowed red in the firelight. "What kind of fool are you to let him out of your sight?"

"Where could he go in this forest? He would not leave the fires."

"Find him," Sard spit out.

Thag stared back at Sard for a few seconds. Then without a word or a sign, he wheeled around to search the camp for Trave.

A warlord, who had been waiting his chance, came up to Sard, bowing nearly to the ground.

Sard turned fully to the man. "Yes?" His voice had the peevish ring of an annoyed child's.

"Congratulations on getting the prince, my lord."

"Thank you," said Sard, appeased.

"Your way will prove best, Master Sard. I have believed so all along," the warlord said.

"You speak as though there is some other choice."

"Not for any loyal Sardan."

"Certainly there can be no disloyal ones." Sard looked keenly at the man.

The soldier said nothing.

Sard weighed his words. "If you were Sard," he said, and looked away into the fire, "which would you think more disloyal—a man who had treason in his heart or one who knew of treason and did not tell of it?"

"There was some talk while you were away, my lord," the man said quickly. "Among some of the warlords."

"Go on."

"Some would rather take Gadalla by force."

"Who brought up this other plan?" Sard demanded.

The other did not answer.

"Who? I warn you," said Sard.

"I do not know."

"Surely there was a leader. Such talk does not come from the smoke of the fires."

After a short silence the warlord said, "Some would call Thag a leader."

Sard dismissed the warlord and ordered two soldiers to stand beside him. They waited for Thag's return.

"The boy sleeps beside a fire," Thag approached Sard. "I have left a soldier to guard him."

Sard made no reply. Thag saw the trap too late.

"Take him!" Sard ordered.

The soldiers grasped Thag before he could move.

"So," said the ruler. "You would be master. Let us see how loyal your men are to you."

Sard strode forward, grabbing up a tar torch from the fire. "Bring him."

The soldiers dragged the underlord behind Sard.

"See here," Sard's voice bellowed through the camp. "Your mighty leader, Thag!"

A few warlords rushed forward. But soldiers loyal to Sard jumped in front of him, swords flashing.

The noise awakened Trave, even though in his weariness he had fallen soundly asleep. He was shocked to see Thag held like some enemy. And he was alarmed by the awful gleam which, even at some distance, he could see in Sard's eyes.

"Now," roared the leader, "now see how brave he acts!"

With that he whirled around and waved the torch close to Thag's face.

The underlord strained away from the flames, but the guards held him fast.

"Let's see the real Thag," said Sard, and laughed, an echoing, hollow laugh without any human sound in it.

Trave was half-crouched by his fire, afraid to move and afraid not to.

And then, to Trave's horror, Thag's face began to melt. The smooth, lineless face gave way like a candle that had burned too long and ran down his tunic. It ran like liquid wax, first in great drops and then in quick little rivers.

Trave sprang to his feet.

One side of Thag's smooth skin had melted completely away. Underneath was a face so horrible that the boy thought he would faint for looking at it.

"Let him go!" ordered Sard. Thag fell to the ground where he covered his face with his hands.

"So there is your would-be leader," hollered Sard to the others. "This is the fate of the man who comes against me!"

Trave broke and ran. But the Sardan soldier came right behind him. The prince made a wild, thrashing run into the forest. Branches tore at him and roots caught at his feet. He flailed at the underbrush, ripping at the limbs that whipped his face. He gasped for breath and stumbled blindly.

And then the soldier overtook him, rolling him to the earth. The man grabbed Trave's arm and hauled him before Sard.

"Well," said Sard. "Two traitors in one night. First the handsome Thag. And now you. Where did you think you would go, boy?" He laughed his terrible laugh.

The guard hauled the prince to a tree and clamped iron bands to his wrists. The bands were hooked through an iron ring and the ring to a heavy chain which circled the tree. Trave fell against the trunk, helpless.

Just a little farther off, Thag sat chained to a tree. Trave could not keep from looking at the real face of the Sardan underlord. It was twisted and grooved like an old tree root and was nearly the same color. Thag looked up. Trave looked away, sickened.

Sard strode back and forth in front of his men. He ranted at them in Sardan, and they trembled before him.

Trave felt fear now as he had never known. He ached for the green hills of Gadalla, for his horse, and for his owl. He almost wished he could feel Gris's hand on his shoulder. He was sure he would not hate it now.

Sard stopped shouting. The only sounds were the snorting and the rumbling of the grelds. For a long time there was no talking, but it was an uneasy, uncomfortable silence. Sard seemed to be waiting, watching for any more challenges to his power. No one moved before him; he paced slowly like a prowling cat.

Trave struggled with the bands on his wrists. He worked them until his skin got raw and red all around the bands. It was hopeless.

CHAPTER 13
Skreels

Hours passed. Trave was not sure how many. His injured wrists throbbed.

The silence in the camp had gone unbroken. Sard, in his fury, had forgotten all else. He was determined to grind all resistance under the heel of his iron boot.

Outside the forest it was nearly noon. Animals and birds everywhere were returning for the day to their dens and perches, their night's hunting done. From the Rudus Desert, the giant birds of prey for which Skreel Forest was named flew back. Their talons full of food from the night's hunt, they passed low over the desert and plunged into the forest, screeching. There were hundreds of them, each one six times the size of Umbo. The birds swooped deep into their forest.

At Sard's camp, the men had begun to sit down in groups, to await Sard's word. They still did not speak but poked into the fires with long sticks. The grelds were quieter now. Trave sat still, trying not to put any weight on his wrists.

At first the sound seemed far away, like sheets flapping in the wind. And then it got louder and louder, and suddenly the flapping was everywhere overhead, everywhere around the camp.

"Skreels!" several men cried at once. The soldiers grabbed for their bows and for their axes and swords.

The huge birds, with their crooked beaks and their purple-black feathers, dived down at the running men. They screeched as they plunged, enraged by the light and smoke of the fires and the sight of men. Near the fires, their feathers flashed with many colors.

Sard's men swung at the diving birds. Here and there a bird wheeled back upward, screaming. But many more streamed downward toward the men.

Trave clung as tightly to the tree as he could. He hardly had the courage to look up. All at once he heard a terrible screech. His head jerked back, and there, headed straight for him, came a skreel, talons down and spread wide.

Trave yelled in fright, and, with strength he did not know he had, he yanked the iron ring to the other side of the tree. The chain ground into the trunk, and the bands sliced his arms. The skreel struck the tree and flew upward. Again it dived at Trave.

This time a soldier caught the monster with an axe, and the skreel fell in a purple pile at Trave's feet.

It seemed to keep screaming even in death, and then Trave realized that it was his own scream he heard.

The birds came on, dozens of them. Again and again they attacked the men. A few fell to the weapons of the Sardans. Most gave up the attack by and by and flew to some other part of the forest, their screeching dying away.

Then there was silence.

The prince slumped weakly down into his bonds. "Oh, Gris," he heard himself saying, "I know what is true. I know what is true. What a fool I am." Over and over he said to himself, "I know what is true."

Sard crawled out from under the exposed roots where he had been hiding. He looked around his camp. Wounded men lay here and there.

"Harness the grelds!" he roared. "We move now!"

Soldiers ran to put the trappings on the great lizards. Others tried to help the fallen men.

"Move!" Sard ordered. "Move, move!"

Camp was broken, and the guard made ready to ride. The ruler ordered Trave brought to him.

"You walk for punishment," he said. The soldiers slipped the ring of Trave's wristbands over a hooked pole and handed the pole to Sard. Then they clamped the hook shut with a loud snap.

"What about the wounded?" asked a warlord near the front.

"Those that can ride will ride," said Sard.

"And those that cannot?"

Sard climbed onto the platform, drawing the iron tail ring up as he did. "Leave them," he said. He heaved the tail ring of his greld upward, and the beast sprang forward with a roar.

Trave looked back in pity at the soldiers unable to ride. As he stumbled past them, trying to keep up with the greld, he heard them call out in Sardan. One of the men left behind was the warlord who had warned Sard of treason. Another was Thag.

The Sardans moved on without stopping. Trave stumbled along behind Sard's animal.

It was late day when they broke from Skreel Forest. They headed south toward the Malus Sea. The grelds roared and squealed when hit on the neck. The beasts did not move as fast as a horse trots, or Trave would never have been able to stay on his feet as long as he did.

At last the Sardans stopped to eat. Trave, having not slept for more than a few minutes in two days and having eaten nothing since Nog's brown bread, fell to the earth where he stood. His wrists hurt, his mouth was dry, he was sick, and his head swam.

The prince lay among the grelds, not caring whether they stepped on him. The Sardans moved off a little to eat their raw meat. They did not bother to post a guard over a boy who could not stand up. They became sluggish after a while, the battle with the skreels and the hard ride undoing them. They loosened their boots and sprawled about on the ground.

Trave called out in a fever, but no Sardan heard. At least no one bothered to look about him. His head and all his bones ached. He was hot, unbearably hot. He rolled about in his misery.

"Gris," he mumbled, and he might have cried had he had the strength. "Gris."

From very close beside him, he heard a voice he knew well, speaking in Gadallan. "Look here, Trave."

The prince turned toward the voice and opened his eyes. It was the King of Kapnos.

CHAPTER 14
Another Dideran

Gris carried Trave to Cene. Then he went, silent as a shadow, to the grelds and pulled the chains out of their tail rings, prodding the animals to move off and discover that they were free. He came swiftly back to Trave and away they rode, north to Dider. Cene ran smoothly and swiftly, like a river without rocks. He tracked fleetly across Rudus Desert with ease.

When they were a long, safe distance from the Sardans, the king set up camp for the night. He made a comfortable bed for Trave and cooked a rich broth. He helped the prince sit up and drink the broth. Then he took out a small silver tool and worked at the hinges of the iron bands on Trave's wrists. He turned the tool slowly, slowly so as not to make the bands move against the boy's wounded wrists. Trave watched as first one, and then the other, band hinge gave way. Gris carefully opened the bands and lifted them off.

Trave's head began to be less dizzy.

"Gris," he said, "I have learned what is true."

"Hush, son," said the old man. "Tomorrow."

He washed the wounds and spread a creamy white ointment over Trave's hands and much of his arms. Then he wrapped a loosely woven cloth over the wounds. Last he drew a cover over the prince.

"Sleep now," the deep, full voice said.

Trave needed not to be told. He fell immediately into a heavy, dreamless sleep.

It was early morning when Trave awoke. He realized that he was moving, and then he saw that he was sitting on Cene in front of Gris. Lenap trotted alongside, his reins tied to the horn of Cene's saddle.

"Where are we?" he asked.

"In Dider," said the king.

He stopped then to let Trave wash and eat.

"Do you feel better?" he asked the prince.

Trave nodded. "Thank you, sir." Then he looked fully at the king. "I'm sorry."

"Do you know what the second duty of a king is, Trave?"

Trave did not.

"The second duty of a king is to believe the truth."

"I believe it," said Trave.

"I'm sure you do," said Gris. "You have come to the truth in a hard, foolish way. But you have come to it."

Trave looked down at his bandaged wrists.

"We will ride on to Kapnos for my army," said the king. "Now that Sard has no prince for the people of Gadalla, he will try whatever he can to take your country. And after Gadalla, Kolonia."

Trave felt as if there were stones in his chest. "I'm sorry," he said again.

"I know, Trave," said Gris. "Now let us get on with what must be done."

"What is to be done?" Trave asked, thinking of his people and of the Kolonian governor's wife with her golden hair.

"We shall defend Gadalla," said the king. "Tanarad has already taken men to hold the borders until we come."

Trave was ashamed. He understood now what pain was, and he knew that Tanarad had been hurt far worse than he. "Is Tanarad well now?"

"His wounds are healed, but his hearing has not improved," said Gris. "But he will protect your country until we get there. Let us ride."

Trave rode Lenap. In a little while, Umbo passed overhead.

"Umbo!" Trave called out. "Umbo!"

The owl swung around and dipped his wing to show he heard. "What a fine bird," said Trave. He smiled.

Gris smiled, too. "Indeed he is."

"Lenap is a fine horse, too." Trave's relief at being rescued had begun to make him a bit lightheaded.

The prince and the king rode on together until noon. Trave grew tired, and his arms ached. Gris saw how pale the boy had become, and drew Cene up.

"Shall we rest?" he asked.

"I'm fine," Trave answered. "Gadalla is more important. I can make it." Despite his cheerful words, Trave's eyes were dull. Gris turned east toward the Brass Mountains. Trave wondered about the change of direction, but he asked no questions.

The afternoon sun glinted off the shiny sides of the mountains and arced outward in rainbows. A thick, curly moss grew among the crevices and on the flat ridges. It was spotted brightly with tiny deep blue flowers.

"How beautiful," said Trave. He leaned forward a little in his saddle from weariness. His head ached.

Soon they were among the mountains. Small streams and fountains sparkled everywhere. Large red flowers growing low to the ground bobbed brightly in the light wind. The horses stepped along in a thick, close turf.

Presently Gris led the way into a meadow that was just as round as a wedding ring. The air in this little pocket between the mountains was cool and smelled of the nodding red flowers.

Gris dismounted. Trave did so as well. They dropped the reins, and the horses began to graze. Without speaking, the king walked a short distance across the meadow. He motioned for Trave to follow.

Then they sat down. Trave looked to Gris, but the king offered no explanation.

Across the meadow Trave could see what seemed to be a glass arch. It looked to be the mouth of a cave. A rainbow wavered and shimmered around it, a rainbow more vivid than any in the mountains. In a few minutes a woman appeared in the glass arch, and she walked toward the king and the prince.

Trave felt happy at her approach, but he could not tell why. She came on, walking calmly and with authority. She wore a pearl-colored gown under a long, full cape made of some light fabric that floated out and back. From one side of the meadow, a small white deer ran out to meet her. She held its head between her hands a moment, and smiled. Then she motioned the deer away, with so gentle a movement that Trave thought perhaps he had imagined it.

Trave could see her well now. She seemed to be both young and old at once. She did not seem to hurry, but she crossed the meadow with easy swiftness. As she drew close, Trave felt he should stand. He then saw that Gris was already standing.

The lady stopped, her cape billowing softly around her. Her veil covered her hair, but not the top of her head or her face. She smiled at them, and Trave felt more welcome than he had ever felt anywhere. She curtsied deeply to Gris, her rich gown crumpling gracefully around her. She rose again.

She spoke to Gris in a language Trave had not heard in any of his travels. Her voice was lighter than the wind and full of music such as flowed from the stringed instruments of Kolonia.

Gris bowed to her and replied in the same language. Then he motioned to Trave, and Trave heard his name spoken. The king turned to Trave.

"This lady," he said, "is Enna, of the Diderans."

The lady turned her warm gaze upon the prince. Trave remembered the stories on the wall of Ogham Pass, and he could not look away from her face.

"Are you the King of Gadalla?" she asked him, her wonderful voice coming forth in Gadallan.

"I am the prince," he said.

"I see," she said. "And you are hurt?"

"A little," Trave answered. He glanced down at his wrists.

She reached forward, taking one wrist in each of her hands. "This is easily healed," she said to Gris, unwrapping one bandage. "Come with me," she went on, turning again to Trave, circling his shoulders with her arm.

Inside her glass cave all was light. Trave could not tell where the light came from, but it was a lovely, warm light, like sunshine. Along glass shelves with brass fittings sat hundreds of gold and silver bottles with precious gems for stoppers. Several had brilliant emerald stoppers.

Enna took down one of these bottles, and with deft motions swept away Trave's bandages. Then she poured a colorless, sticky liquid over his wrists. Even as he watched, the skin began to heal over. The swelling went down; the redness faded. The ache went almost completely away.

"Thank you," the boy said as relief poured over him. "Thank you." Then a great sleepiness came upon him, like a giant hand weighing him down, and he fell forward. The lady caught him against her shoulder.

When Trave woke up, he felt that he had slept for hours, even days. But it had only been a few seconds that he had leaned against the Dideran lady's shoulder. He pulled back, blinking.

Enna only studied him with gentle looks, waiting for him to look up at her.

Trave's wrists looked as if they had healed years before. Only white scars remained.

"How did you do that?" Trave asked in awe.

She laughed a little as though she had done nothing remarkable.

"Enna knows many things," said Gris.

"Will I always have the scars?" asked Trave.

Enna looked to Gris. The king said nothing, but let the lady follow her own ways.

"Why would you be rid of them?" the lady wanted to know, turning to Trave.

"I got them dishonorably," Trave said.

"Perhaps, then," she said, "they will remind you to be honorable."

Trave gazed sadly down.

"But," she went on in her rich tones, "I do have something special." She got up and went into another room, her voice carrying back to the men. "I have a medicine from the bloom of the pinnell. The pinnell is a rare plant that blossoms only once every seventy years."

She came back with a small white bottle in her palm. "If you take this, you will be cured of anything. It can even dissolve scars."

Trave wanted very much to have the medicine. Enna held it forth to him. The prince took it and looked at it a long time. Then he raised his eyes to hers.

"It can cure anything?"

"It can." She came close to him and held both his wrists up between her hands. She did not look at his scars, however, but directly at him. "But before you act," she said, "consider. Was it not pride that led you to what gave you these scars?"

Trave's face flushed under her steady gaze. How much did she know, he wondered.

The lady went on. "And is it not pride that makes you want to be rid of them?"

He looked at his wrists, for he could not look at her.

"Consider," she said again, "which will be the true cure—to take the medicine, or not to take it?"

"My lady," said Trave, "I will consider."

Enna released his wrists and turned to the king.

Gris rose to leave. He took her hand briefly, carefully. "Again, I am in your debt, lady."

"You honor me by coming," she returned. To Trave she said, "Reign nobly, Prince."

Trave could only nod and bow to her.

Neither Gris nor the prince spoke as they traveled out of the Brass Mountains. Trave looked back once, to remember the way to the round meadow. But the mountains and the ravines all looked the same. The setting sun glowed orange just above them.

At nightfall, they made camp about a half day's ride from Lapis, the largest Dideran city. Umbo came in and perched for the night near Trave.

"Hello, boy," said the prince. Stroking the bird's feathers made him strangely homesick for Gadalla.

He said to Gris, "Thank you for looking after Umbo and Lenap."

"You're welcome," said the king.

Trave did not look at Gris as he said, "I hope we can save Gadalla."

The king said, "Do you believe that what you have learned will help you rule Gadalla well?"

"I do."

"The third duty of a king, Trave, is to act on the truth he has come to believe."

And then it fell dark in Dider.

CHAPTER 15

Revenge

The small fire that Trave had built leaped up, sending skyward little sparks. The prince could just see Umbo's outline on a nearby branch. The bird had his head tucked under his wing. Lenap stood, head drooping, close by.

"Gris," said Trave.

"Yes?"

"Tell me of my father."

The fire snapped quietly. The night birds of Dider called to each other.

"Your father," said the king, "knew every soldier in his army by name. He spoke four languages, and he could get such music from a silver horn as you have never heard."

Gris waited. When Trave said nothing, he went on.

"He told me once that being a king was the most humbling task a man could have."

"Humbling?" asked Trave, with more fear than surprise in his voice.

"He said, 'So many good people to care for, so much trust given to you—who is really worthy?'"

"I am not worthy of my father's medallion."

"Trave," said the king, "leave the past behind now." He broke a stick and threw it into the fire.

"Can I ever be a king like my father?"

"I believe so," said Gris.

Trave felt the small bottle that Enna had given him inside his tunic, but he did not take it out or speak of it.

The stars shone clearly. Most were gold or white. Trave saw one red one.

"Did you know my mother well?"

"I met her a few times before you were born. A gentle, wise lady, she was, with eyes much like the Lady Enna's."

"She died when I was born."

"Soon after."

Trave said no more, and Gris banked the fire for the night.

Both slept. Gris slept more heavily than usual, for he had not rested since he had left Wrycan. Trave, having just been attended by the Dideran lady, slept more lightly, but he slept.

He dreamed of Ganet, his shining capital city. He saw his throne, and around it was an ugly vine, hacked to pieces and withering. All around him, men were crying "War! War!" and he whirled about, looking for Gris. But the king was not there.

His eyes popped open. Had he heard a snap, or had he dreamed it? He listened, his heart pounding. Again the sound came, a dry snap.

Trave eased over to Gris and reached for the king's boot, to shake him. And then in the dim light of the fire and early morning, he saw that the king already stood, his sword half-drawn.

Trave did not move. They listened, and they searched the trees without turning their heads.

Nothing moved anywhere for several seconds.

Then Gris drew out his wonderful sword completely. It seemed to flash with a light of its own. "Come forward, Sard."

From the trees ahead, the Sardan ruler, with his iron helmet and full battle gear, appeared.

"I have come for what is mine," he said. Trave could see him only dimly.

"Go back where you came from," said Gris.

"Gadalla is mine!" Sard's voice echoed through the woods. He came forward, his sword before him.

"I said go back." Gris's voice was hard and cold. Trave stood up beside the king.

Sard came on, but sidling left. Gris turned where he stood to keep facing the Sardan directly.

Sard came closer, little by little. "Give the medallion over. Save yourself a fight, old man." He made little circles with the tip of his sword as he talked. "I'll get it anyway."

Gris's face was set; his eyes never left the Sardan's.

"Come no closer," said Gris.

Sard stopped. He spoke angrily. "Who are you to command me? I am Master of Sarda. The boy and I have a deal. Stay out of my way."

Gris motioned Trave away from the angry Sardan. Trave noticed again how perfectly Sard spoke Gadallan.

Suddenly Sard leaped forward, taking a plunge at the king with his sword.

Gris caught Sard's sword with his and threw the other's arm up and back. The thrust made Sard stumble backward.

He steadied himself and then lunged again. Gris sprang back like a cat. Sard came on once more. Gris met the blow with the edge of his weapon. The crack of blades together sounded through the woods.

Crack! The blades went again, and again, and again. Sard swung well, but Gris stopped every swing with the edge of the sword.

Sard roared with anger and charged at Gris. The king stood his ground. He caught Sard's sword just at the hilt and heaved mightily. Sard fell backward, sprawling, but still holding his weapon. He swung his sword wildly at Gris until he could stand again.

"Now I will fight, old man," he hollered.

He ran at Gris like a wild bear. Gris ducked a blow and swung around. Sard whirled, his eyes flashing. The small firelight just under him glowed on the iron snake of his helmet.

Trave thought what to do. "Umbo!" he called. "Attack!"

There was a sudden rush of wings very near. The great white owl soared up and then straight down at the snake on Sard's helmet, snatching at it.

Sard staggered back, and then, angry, lunged forward at the bird, catching the tip of his sword under one of Umbo's wings. Umbo arced away, screeching.

Sard had showed no fear of the owl, but he was off balance from the attack.

Gris delivered a smashing blow to Sard's sword, and it rattled to the ground. The Sardan dived for it, but Gris caught his wrist with his foot. Sard tried to pull away, but the old king was stronger.

Gris jerked him up and threw him against a tree, holding him pinned with one powerful hand.

"You are no Sardan. Who are you?" Gris demanded.

The man turned away his face.

"Answer!" Gris demanded.

"Gelu." The man whipped his gaze back to Gris. "Gelu of Gadalla. The man you tried to ruin!"

The king grabbed the man and thrust him back toward the fire with contempt.

"The Gadallan captain! I ought to kill you where you stand."

He glared at the traitor with such fury that Trave imagined that the man would catch fire from the king's anger.

"I should have had the medallion!" Gelu exclaimed. Rage overcame him. "It was to be mine! I was second in command!"

"You were stripped of command!"

"Because of you!" the man roared.

"Because of your lust for power!" Gris roared back.

"I have as much right to power as you!"

Gris bore down on him. "You have no rights. You are a traitor and a usurper!"

"Sarda would be nothing if I had not gained control! I know how to rule—and how to win!"

Suddenly an eerie whistle passed over the fire like a thought. Before any could understand, an arrow, sure and straight, caught Sard in the back of the neck. He dropped like a stone.

Gris sprang in front of Trave, and they both dropped to the ground.

"What happened?" Trave stared at the fallen Sardan just a little in front of them.

"I expect Sarda has a new ruler," said Gris, looking into the trees.

"One of Sard's own men?"

Gris searched the trees but could see nothing. "None of my men would take a man from behind and with no warning."

"Then it was Thag," said Trave. "Sard melted away his mask in front of the Sardan guard. Sard left him to die after the skreels attacked."

They waited, motionless, for some time.

"Is he gone?" asked Trave.

"Could be," said Gris. "but we will wait a little longer."

"But why would he leave us here? What does it mean if he's gone?"

"It means that he does not want you—or the medallion. And that means he will ride against Gadalla to take it by force."

Trave felt grieved that he had helped to bring such trouble to his people.

"There will be war," said Trave. "What should we do?"

"We must get our armies to Gadalla first, before any of the Dark Alliance forces get there," said Gris.

When they finally felt safe enough to stand up, the sun had risen. It shone in clear ribbons through the trees.

The king put his hand on Trave's shoulder, and together the king and the prince walked ahead to a small clearing where the sun poured fully down. It was a brilliant dawn, cloudless and sparkling. They stood in its warmth.

"Trave," said the king. "Gadalla needs a leader. I can return to lead."

"Yes, sir," said Trave without pause.

"But I would rather you did."

Gris then opened his shirt and drew a heavy silver chain over his head. At the end of the chain hung a great medallion. It flashed in the sun.

Trave felt the truth before he heard it. "Is that—?"

"Your father's royal medallion. Now it is yours." Gris put the chain over Trave's head. He felt the weight of it and the pull of the medallion.

"You had it all the time?" Trave asked Gris, looking at the treasure.

Gris nodded. "Yes, I did. Your father said, 'Keep this until Trave can wear it well. If he cannot wear it, give it to the man who can.'"

"You could have been king any time." Trave looked up in wonder at the old man.

The King of Kapnos smiled down. "Gadalla does not need me. It has a king."

Trave fingered the medallion. On the front was a raised picture of Ganet, as it looked from the west hills. On the back were these words, in beautiful Gadallan script:

To learn what is true
To believe the truth
To act on that belief

"Thank you," said Trave quietly. "Thank you."

MEDALLION

"You must prove yourself worthy. You must be a king and do a king's duty."

Trave stood straight and tall before Gris. "I will, sir."

Gris said, "I will ride on to get my army. You must return to Gadalla and call your army together."

Trave said, "As you say, sir."

"Take that sword." Gris pointed to Sard's sword. "Go to Wrycan. Tell the governor what has happened and what you will do." Trave nodded.

"Follow the red star. When it is in line with the three bright gold ones, you are going toward Wrycan. During the day keep the sun passing over you."

"Yes, sir," said Trave.

"Lose no time, Trave. We have none to spare."

"Umbo—" Trave began.

"If he is here, I will find him," said Gris. "Now ride. And remember, you are a king."

Trave saddled his horse, saluted Gris, and rode away.

Gris set about to bury his enemy.

CHAPTER 16
The Return

Trave galloped Lenap away from the Brass Mountains. At first he rode without thinking of anything but that he must hurry. He felt the power of the horse under him and remembered to stay easy in the saddle. He gave Lenap a lot of rein.

By and by he began to think of other things. The terrible screech that Umbo had made when his wing was torn sounded in his ears. He heard again the deadly skreels and felt the horror of their dives at him. And then he thought of the girl in Ganet whom Umbo had frightened, and he was truly sorry he had called her a coward.

The land of Dider passed swiftly beneath his horse. The sun moved high overhead and, after long hours, dropped in the sky behind him.

Trave dismounted near a stream to let Lenap drink and rest. Long afternoon shadows fell around him. The air grew cooler.

For some time he walked, leading his horse. When it got dark, he found his red star and followed it. He rode again.

Just at daybreak, Trave crossed the border into Torus Point. Again he got off and walked, letting Lenap rest a bit. He could see no streams or pools here, no matter where he looked.

"I'm sorry, boy," he said to his horse.

Trave was thirsty himself, and he began to get hungry. He did not consider, however, stopping to find something. He walked for a long time.

The sun bore down on the short, brown grass of Torus Point. Trave thought of shade and cool water, but he kept walking.

Toward afternoon, he remounted. This time he asked only a trot from Lenap.

The sun went down a second time on the pair. This time when Trave got down, he took off the saddle and let Lenap graze what little he could on the tough grass.

Trave himself sprawled on the ground and fell asleep. He awoke with a start, hunger chewing at him. The stars were bright overhead. He hoped he had not lost too much time.

Sometime after the sun came up, Trave found a stream that ran into the north end of Blee Bog. Both he and Lenap drank deeply of the clear water. Trave remembered with shame the last time he had come this way. The Bog looked far less horrible in the day.

On the Kolonian side the grass was higher and sweeter. Trave let his horse eat a little, and then he set off again. His body ached all over from hunger and weariness. He slumped forward over Lenap's neck.

And then he fell off. He lay upon the ground, too weak to move.

Get up, he told himself.

He managed to come to his knees. Holding Lenap's reins, he hauled himself to his feet. He leaned against the horse, his face in its neck.

"You are the king," he thought. "You are *the king.*"

He looked around. Far ahead he saw a small hut with sheep in a field beside it. Too weary to mount his horse, he stumbled forward.

What would he say to anyone? He was dirty. His clothes were torn. His eyes were tired and sore.

No one was about the hut. Trave called hoarsely, but no one answered. He went inside, still calling. There was bread on the rough-cut table.

Trave sat down, and after a moment, ate the bread. He cut himself some cheese and drank from a pitcher. He began to feel better. The hut was furnished with rough wooden stools and heavy hand-built pottery. It was well swept and airy. Trave remembered the boy Volar and his family and wondered if he had lived in such a house as this. He took off a ring, worth hundreds of such small meals as he had just eaten, and laid it on the table.

With this rest and food, he traveled on.

Some long time later, Trave did not even know which day, he entered the west gate of Wrycan. The gatekeepers ran forward to help him, fearing he would fall.

"See to my horse, if you will," he said, as he slid off, exhausted.

At the governor's hall, Trave ate and drank and slept. When he finally stood before the governor, he wore the fine mesh mail and the sword that Gris had ordered made for him. He had new clothes, a gift from the governor. His boots had been shined, and he was clean. His medallion hung heavy and shiny on his chest.

"Governor," he said, "Sard is dead."

The governor looked astonished.

"Gris thinks some underlord, probably Thag, will move his army against Gadalla," Trave went on, "and then against Kolonia."

"Very likely," said the governor. "Tanarad already has the Kolonian army and the royal guard of Kapnos along our border."

"Sir," said Trave, "I request a horse. I will return for Lenap as soon as I can." He spoke Kolonian.

"A fine horse is already saddled and waiting," returned the governor.

"Thank you," Trave said. "Could you send word to Tanarad to bring his troops into Gadalla—to Ganet?"

"It will be done." The governor nodded to one of his men. The man went out.

Trave said, "I am in your debt."

"Live long and well," said the governor.

Trave bowed deeply and went out to do his duty.

At dusk the second day, Trave reached the Saum River at Ogham Pass. There were no barges, but several young Kolonians stood by.

"Do you know Tanarad?" Trave asked them.

One man nodded.

"When Tanarad comes, please say that Trave of Gadalla has passed over the river."

They bowed, and Trave guided his horse into the river. He held his fine new sword high out of the water. It glinted in the fading sun.

The current pushed against the horse, but Trave tapped him lightly all the while. The horse swam well. When he pulled up on the far bank, Trave looked back on the way he had come. It was quickly growing dark. Trave ran his eye along the Kolonian wall. He determined to learn every language on it, to know all the legends written there.

He passed by in the gathering dusk. The wall ended, and Trave knew he was home again.

Darkness covered the land. Trave wanted to ride straight on to Ganet, but he felt his horse flagging. He stopped to rest.

In the stillness, he could faintly hear voices. He strained to listen. They seemed to come from just a little north of him. He walked toward the voices.

As he came closer, he heard his own language. Soon he saw a small fire and could make out three or four men standing by it.

He stopped safely back from them to listen.

"It's been five years," said one voice.

"Five years or fifty," said another, "it matters not."

"One of us," said the first again, "should have spoken to Gris when he was here."

"He could only tell us what we already know: our duty is to wait for the rightful king."

"And so we do," said one who had not yet spoken. "And so do all loyal Gadallans—soldiers and citizens."

Trave came forward then, leading his horse.

"Are you Gadallan soldiers?" he asked.

The men spun around from the fire.

"Who asks?"

"Trave of Gadalla."

"Prince Trave!" said two soldiers at once.

"Welcome, Prince," said the first man.

Trave walked ahead into their little circle of light. His medallion as it swung against his chest caught the firelight briefly.

There was an awed silence.

"Sir," the oldest man finally said, "what medallion do you wear?"

Trave held it forth. "My father's."

Every man bowed low to the ground.

"Please," said Trave, "rise. I have much to ask you."

"Your Majesty," said the first soldier. "We are grateful you have come. Gadalla is in great need of a king."

"With your permission, Your Grace," said another, "we would do a duty we have waited five years to do!"

"Granted," said the king.

Joyfully, the men thrust torches into the fire. They brought them out blazing and ran to light a huge bonfire. The dry sticks and brush in the great pile burst instantly into flame. The whole sky was lit with it. The men cheered, clapping each other's shoulders and stomping with much gladness.

Only a few minutes passed before one man called out to the others.

On a distant hill another fire had sprung up, and then another, and another. Soon bonfires flared in lines across the hills as far as Trave could see. The hills shimmered with the fires, hundreds of them.

"What is this?" asked the king.

"Your soldiers, Your Majesty. We wait your command."

"All of these?" said Trave.

"Your people, Your Grace, faithful and ready," said the old one.

For a moment the new king could not speak. At last he said, "Gadalla is in great danger from Sarda. We must defend her." He paused. "We should ride south of Ganet, for surely the enemy will come up from the south. We must stop them before they reach the capital." He waited, then, for them to speak.

The oldest soldier stepped up respectfully. "That seems best, sir." The man's gray beard hung nearly to his belt.

"Agreed?" Trave asked the rest.

"Yes, sir," they said.

"Then let us ride." He swung onto his horse, waiting.

"Quickly," said the old soldier. "The king is ready."

"Do you have signals prepared?" asked Trave.

"We do, Your Grace."

"Well done," the king said. "Send them."

A little past daybreak, Trave's whole army swept into the plain south of Ganet—men and horses, battle gear and harness. They halted at their king's word, which was relayed through the army by the shouts of the captains. Trave sat on his horse, waiting. The day moved on, and nothing happened.

The next morning the men took their full positions again. The king sat on his horse in the morning sun. An outrider galloped up to Trave and saluted.

"Sir, Tanarad of Kapnos comes with a great army."

Trave's heart rose for joy. "Tell him to bring his army west and south. Ask him to meet me here."

The rider saluted and rode off.

Trave drew the bottle that Enna had given him from his tunic. He turned it round and round thoughtfully. He looked at the scars on his wrists for a long time, considering the words the lady had spoken.

Tanarad brought his horse beside Trave's. His arm was still in a sling. His eyes fell at once on the medallion.

"Your most noble highness," he said. "I am at your service."

"Tanarad," said Trave, "I am glad to see you. I need your advice."

Together they rode a short way off.

"Gris comes behind," said Trave, "with the Kapnos army."

Tanarad nodded, watching Trave's mouth to help himself sort out the words.

"Sard is dead," Trave went on. "I believe Thag killed him."

Tanarad looked surprised but asked no questions.

"Are we doing what is best here?" he asked the captain.

"Indeed, Your Grace."

Trave nodded, thoughtful. He glanced at the captain, who carried himself like a soldier despite his injuries. At last Trave spoke.

"You have been a great friend to Gadalla—even when you might well have gone home to rest."

Tanarad made ready to answer, but Trave put up his hand.

"No. You have done Gadalla much service. I have brought you a gift."

He held out the small bottle.

"Your Grace?"

"Something that Enna of the Diderans gave me and that I now give you."

"The Lady Enna!" said the captain. "Your Highness, what a gift this is!" He paused. "I do not deserve such generosity."

"I owe you," said Trave.

"Sir, I do my duty. My orders—"

"For riding lessons," the new king said.

Tanarad smiled. "I am overpaid."

Trave smiled back. "Then let us say I prefer to have my fellow commanders in good health."

Tanarad took the shining bottle. "Thank you, Your Grace. A thousand and a thousand thanks."

Trave nodded and then urged his horse ahead and rode back to his position in front of the army. Now, he thought, all is cleared.

Late in the afternoon, a thin line of dust appeared on the horizon far to the south. Trave and Tanarad stood side by side, holding their hands above their eyes to see better. Tanarad's sling was gone, and his face showed no bruises.

"The Sardan army," said Tanarad. "I hear the screaming of the grelds."

"How long until they come close enough for battle?"

"Tomorrow morning," said the captain, and Trave nodded slowly.

Morning came, but the Sardans did not.

"Perhaps," said Tanarad, "their outriders have seen the size of our army, and the Sardans will turn back."

Trave was not sure. "Perhaps. Command the men to gear for battle," said the young king.

Tanarad said, "Yes, sir," and swung onto his horse.

Everywhere men began to harness their horses and armor themselves. They clamped chamfrons to the horses' heads and strapped on the flank shields and the neck bards. The leather creaked, and the metal clanked and rang. Then the men put on their own chest pieces, their helmets, their thick leather gloves, and hefted their shields from the battle wagons.

Sooner than he thought it possible, Trave gazed out at his army, fitted for war and waiting.

In two hours, however, a vast line of soldiers appeared over the rise. The iron-booted soldiers halted their grelds at the crest. In front on horseback rode Thag and six of his captains. They came on within shouting range and stopped.

The leaders of both armies faced each other tensely.

"Surrender!" roared Thag.

Trave, his new mail gleaming, urged his horse ahead one step.

"Get out of Gadalla!" he shouted.

"Ha, ha, ha!" laughed Thag. "What did you say, little boy?"

Thag and his six men came forward a little more.

"Why not spare all those men, little boy?"

"Every man behind me will die before a murderer is king in Gadalla!" Trave shouted. "Turn back, or we will drive you into the sea!"

Thag stood up in his stirrups. "Have it your way!" he roared, and swung his horse violently around.

Trave called to Tanarad, "Prepare for battle!"

Tanarad called to his captains. The Kolonians, the Gadallans, and the Kapnos guard drew out their swords, bows, and axes.

The cry began. "Save Gadalla! Save Gadalla!" It ran through every line of soldiers and thundered up from the plain, five thousand voices strong. "Save Gadalla!"

Trave, sitting on his horse, said softly to himself, "Save Gadalla."

CHAPTER 17
The Battle and What Came After

Tanarad called to Trave, "Withdraw to the northeast rise, Your Highness. Command from there."

Trave said, "No, I will fight."

The captain rode close. "With respect, Your Grace, you do your men a disservice by staying."

"How is that?"

"A king commands, rallies. Only when the battle is sore does the king himself ride in. It is the way of things."

Trave held out one second more.

"The battle," said Tanarad, "may come to you. Let us hope it does not."

"Send messengers at every turn of battle," said Trave, and he spurred his horse northeastward.

"I will, Your Grace," Tanarad called after him.

The front lines of both armies received the command to attack. They launched forward, the Sardans on their grelds and the Gadallans and their allies on horseback, each line bellowing war cries.

Tanarad swung west along the Gadallan ranks. He called commands as he rode. The thunder of horses and grelds filled the plains. From the rise Trave saw the two lines crash together, and he heard the awful roll and rumble of a battle beginning.

The steely ring of sword on sword and the warbling clang of battle axe on shield sounded above the snorting of the horses and the shouting of the soldiers. Arrows fell in sheets from both directions, and the dust of the plains rose up in clouds on every hand. Both lines drew back momentarily and then came on again.

The Gadallans, skilled in war, unseated Sardan after Sardan with deft blows of their long, heavy lances. The battle horses snorted and squealed at the grelds but did not rear nor turn aside. The Sardans beat the necks of the animals to move them ahead, the grelds' sheer bulk overwhelming the horses.

A fresh volley of arrows rained down on the Gadallans, who threw shields up against the shower. At Tanarad's command a line of Kolonian archers advanced, shooting over the heads of their comrades into the ranks of the Sardans. The Gadallan front line lunged ahead as the Sardans raised their shields against the arrows, toppling many Sardans from their grelds.

The Gadallans would have advanced, but Tanarad held them.

"Soldier," he called to a man near him. "Ride to King Trave. Tell him I want to bring up the Kapnos guard to the west to hold the Sardans back. Ride, man!"

The messenger flew to Trave with the words.

The king said, "Say to the captain he may do howsoever he sees fit. How goes the battle?"

"The Sardans have not crossed our line of defense, but they are not dropping back either."

Trave said, "Send me a man to carry messages. Ride on."

The clash sounded from the plains again, and the dust billowed up. Tanarad ordered the royal guard west.

Thag bellowed to one of his men, "Kapnos soldiers to the west! Bring a third rank parallel."

The man hesitated. "It is the royal guard—see the banner!"

Thag struck him with a riding stick. "Bring up the rank! When the Torridians come, we will crush the guard between us!"

The soldier fled, his ear bleeding.

As the sun rose straight overhead, the battle raged on. There were no longer two lines on the plain, but a huge expanse of battling men. Nearly half of both armies clashed on the field. Neither side gave ground.

Thag paced around on his frothing horse. One of his captains stood awaiting his orders. An outrider, on horseback, also waited.

"You're sure there are no Diderans?" Thag demanded.

"We have seen none," said the outrider.

"Surely they will come," Thag said, turning his horse into a tight circle. "We must be in command by nightfall, or the Diderans will destroy us."

"Where is rest of the Kapnos army?" asked the Sardan soldier.

Thag ignored him. "Look!" he cried.

To the northwest, riding in great numbers, came the black-masked Torridians.

"Now we have the enemy!" Thag said. "Bolster the rank against the royal guard of Kapnos. Crush that guard and we crush an army!"

The Torridians came on, pouring out of the northwest toward the battlefield. Trave saw the danger from his vantage point.

"Find Tanarad of Kapnos—among the royal guard—warn him!" he said to his messenger. The man galloped away as though an arrow followed him.

But he arrived with his news too late for Tanarad to move the guard. The Torridians closed in. Horrified, Trave sprang into the saddle to ride into the field. And then, as if he dreamed, as if wishes had taken mortal shape, he beheld a most wondrous sight.

Like stars coming out at night, Gris and all his army began to appear along the hills behind the Gadallan and Kolonian armies—and behind the Torridians. On and on they came, hundreds and thousands of soldiers in black and silver, streaming down to the plains, the flags of Kapnos flying.

Trave shouted for joy.

Too late the Torridians discovered their new enemy. They tried to fight on both fronts, but surrounded by Kapnos warriors, they gave way and broke rank. They fled westward and south to join the Sardans.

Thag called up his whole army and, with the Torridians, rode headlong into battle against the opposing army.

The thunder that rose up then shook the very hills. The roar was like some great ocean that had burst up through the Gadallan plains.

All afternoon the battle continued, clash upon clash. At times Trave could not tell one army from another. The flags could not show their colors through the clouds of dust. The sun began to sink in the sky. Slowly, the allies of Gadalla began to push the enemy back.

Trave began to have hope. He imagined the end coming, the cheers of the victors. And then, with a feeling of being drowned, he saw, coming up from the southeast, another army. Litoris had arrived.

Trave felt an awful despair wash over him.

"Your Highness!"

Trave started and turned. It was the gray-bearded soldier he had met at the signal fire days before.

The man spoke on. "A messenger to the King of Kapnos was struck and fell from his horse near me. He repeated the message to me. Sir, I did not know where King Gris was, but I knew where you were. And so, Your Grace, with your permission—"

"Granted," said Trave.

"The Diderans have come through Ogham Pass and ride full out to battle."

Trave jerked his head up to look at the Litoris force.

"You have done well," he told the man. "How do you ride?"

The man looked down. "Not well—not as well as a young man, Your Grace." He looked up. "But I will ride as best I can to serve you."

The man looked older than Gris, full of years and battle wisdom.

"Stand here for me," said Trave. "Stand in my place until I return."

"Your Grace!" The old man was thunderstruck.

"Be a king for two hours, sir, for the sake of Gadalla." With that, Trave leaped into his saddle and rode east like thunder.

He met the Dideran army halfway and turned his horse to gallop among the leaders.

"Swing south," he yelled in Kolonian over the pounding of the hooves. He did not speak Dideran, and he hoped his Kolonian was understandable. "Litoris has come! Get behind them!"

The Diderans saw the medallion that banged against the young king's chest, and they did not doubt him. They turned their lathered horses to follow Trave's order.

Trave rode south with the Dideran army until nearly dusk. Then he pulled west to take up his position on the rise above the battlefield. The Diderans rode on, their longbows silhouetted against the darkening sky.

———

The armies on the plain strove until the sun went down and darkness held the land. At full dark, the fighting stopped. It stopped gradually, the clamor diminishing until all was quiet.

No fires were built, no horses or grelds were unharnessed. The armies drew back a little from each other to wait for morning.

Here and there a horse snorted or armor clanked. Men spoke quietly, if they spoke at all. The stillness was almost more terrifying than the roar of battle. There was a faint light from a sliver of moon. Many men loosened their armor and rested.

Then, ringing out over the quiet, came a voice, first in Sardan, then in Torridian, then in Kolonian and Gadallan: "We are the Diderans!"

A murmur of joy swept through half the hearers; a shudder of terror, through the other half.

Thag stood up, carefully, silently. None of his men moved or spoke.

"We have Gadallan prisoners," he called out. "We will kill them!"

"Surrender," came the answer.

Without speaking Thag moved swiftly away to a new position. He found a wounded Gadallan and drew his Sardan sword. It made the tiniest swish as he did so.

Through the darkness and the quiet came an arrow, instant and sure. Thag fell upon the ground, his helmet and sword clattering.

Terror spread through the Sardans and erupted in chaos. Every man clambered for his armor, his weapons, his greld. They rushed toward the place where the Dideran had spoken. Then Dideran arrows began to rain from afar on the armies of the Dark Alliance. In confusion and panic, they fell upon each other, Sardan attacking Sardan, men of Litoris striking at men of Sarda.

The Kolonians and the Gadallans stood silent in their places, hearing the clank and the thud of weapons and the shouts and the cries of the enemy. Gris's men sat upon their horses, not riding forward, not so much as a step.

Dideran arrows came thick and fast. No other people could string and shoot arrows as quickly as Diderans. Again and again they plied their bows; again and again the arrows fell.

Toward morning, the clamor lessened and at last died away. The Diderans unstrung their bows and waited for the dawn.

When the sun rose, Trave strained to see in the early light. The enemy soldiers were scattered, their armor and their weapons spread like seeds in a plowed field. He saw the Kolonians and the Gadallans starting to move. He saw the Diderans coming in, leading their horses. And then he saw Gris, riding Cene, coming through his army to the battlefield before them.

Both Trave and the gray-bearded soldier who had stood with him mounted their horses and rode down to the plain.

Every man looked about him in wonder. And suddenly the truth of victory was upon them. A cheer started, and it became a roar that swelled and rose and carried like a song of glory to the hills.

Gris and Trave grasped arms in the manner of kings. Tanarad came; Trave and Gris saluted him, and he rode with them like a king.

———

In the evening of the day after the battle, Tanarad, Gris, and Trave, as well as many of the Kolonian and Dideran captains, met at a large fire.

Gris praised the men for their bravery and leadership. Trave thanked them for their help, a sacrifice of which he felt himself unworthy but for which Gadalla would be forever grateful. "Bring every man to Ganet where I shall reward him for his service to my country!"

The captains thanked him heartily.

"Tomorrow, then, at sunrise," said Gris, "we ride to Ganet, at the invitation of the noble King of Gadalla."

When all the men had left, Trave looked at Gris.

"My only concern now," said the young king, "is Panii."

"I'm rather sure he will surrender," said Gris.

And surrender he did. The fat would-be king ran to meet Trave outside the gates the next morning, throwing himself on the ground.

"Have mercy, Your Grace," he said from the dirt. "Have mercy."

Said Trave, "Get up and walk before me."

Panii did so, all the way to the gates.

The gatekeeper swung open the gates, calling, "Welcome, Your Majesty! Welcome, King Trave!"

Beside the gate stood a Kolonian, holding the reins of Lenap.

"Lenap!" said Trave.

"Our governor sends you your horse, sir, with his sincere gratitude for our safety," said the young man.

Trave dismounted. He handed the reins of his Kolonian horse to the gatekeeper. "King's groom," he said, "please see to the governor's horse." He had remembered his promise to the gatekeeper, which seemed to him now so long ago.

"Thank you, King Trave. Thank you," the overjoyed man said.

"And sir," the Kolonian spoke again. "This fine browband on your horse's bridle is a gift from Volar, a harness-maker's apprentice. He says to thank you for remembering him to the governor."

The browband was richly tooled and skillfully polished. Trave smiled widely.

To the Kolonian, in Kolonian, Trave said, "Please thank your governor and Volar. And thank *you*. Live long and well."

He mounted Lenap, easily, like one long familiar with horses.

"Are you not left without a gatekeeper?" asked Gris.

Trave smiled and shook his head. "No. There is a loyal and wise soldier with a gray beard who no longer rides horses who will make a fine gatekeeper."

"And what of Panii?" asked Tanarad.

"Panii," said Trave, "will serve in my kitchen rather than just eat from it. And he will be forced to learn a trade—stable sweeping, I think."

Gris laughed. And Tanarad laughed. And Trave motioned his company on into Ganet.

He rode through the streets to the cheers of his people, his medallion bright and round against his chest. He nodded and waved and turned often to Gris to say how fine a people Gadallans were.

A familiar shadow passed over him, and he looked up. "Ah! Umbo! You are yet alive." The bird flew easily, white against the blue sky. Trave turned to Gris. "Has he been with the Lady Enna?"

But Gris only smiled.

Halfway to the palace, Trave saw among the crowds a girl with thick golden braids wrapped around her head. She was the girl that he had called a coward. He stopped the procession before her.

She curtsied deeply.

"Do you sing?" he asked her.

She blushed. "Yes, your grace, I do."

"Then you must come and sing for us in the palace."

She smiled and curtsied to him again, overcome with the honor.

Then Trave rode on toward the palace and the Great Hall of Gadalla, where he reigned as king for many, many years. The scribes recorded in the books of the Gadallan kings all his brave, true deeds. And in all the history of Gadalla was there never such a king as Trave.

Pronunciation Guide

Places

Brankus   (brănk′əs)

Clar   (klär)

Cordus   (kōrd′əs)

Dag   (dăg)

Dider   (dē′dər)

Fidere   (fī dār′)

Ganet   (găn′ĭt)

Kapnos   (kăp′nōs)

Kolonia   (kə lō′nē ə)

Lapis   (lăp′ĭs)

Litoris   (lĭ tōr′ĭs)

Malus   (măl′əs)

Ogham   (äg′əm)

Regner   (rĕg′nər)

Rubrum   (rōō′br əm)

Sarda   (särd′ə)

Saum   (sôm)

Torridia   (tōr rĭd′ē ə)

Wrycan   (rī′kən)

Characters

Cene   (sēn)

Enna   (ĕn′ə)

Gelu   (gĕl′ōō)

Gris   (grĭs)

Lenap   (lĕn′əp)

Nog   (näg)

Panii   (păn ī′)

Sard   (särd)

Tanarad   (tăn′ə răd′)

Thag   (thăg)

Trave   (trāv)

Umbo   (ŭm′bō)

Volar   (vō lär′)